24 Hours
That Changed the World

24 Hours That Changed the World

For more information, visit www.AdamHamilton.com.

Also by Adam Hamilton

Christianity and World Religions
Christianity's Family Tree
Confronting the Controversies
Creed
Enough
Final Words from the Cross
Forgiveness
Half Truths
John
Leading Beyond the Walls
Love to Stay
Making Sense of the Bible

Not a Silent Night
Revival
*Seeing Gray in a
    World of Black and White*
Selling Swimsuits in the Arctic
Speaking Well
The Call
The Journey
The Way
Unleashing the Word
When Christians Get It Wrong
Why?

ADAM HAMILTON

24 Hours

That Changed the World

— 40 DAYS OF REFLECTION —

Abingdon Press | Nashville

24 HOURS THAT CHANGED THE WORLD:
40 DAYS OF REFLECTION

ISBN 978-1-7910-2631-8

First edition published in 2009 as ISBN 978-1-426-70031-6.

21 22 23 24 25 26 27 28 29 30—10 9 8 7 6 5 4 3 2 1
MANUFACTURED IN THE UNITED STATES OF AMERICA

Contents

Introduction:
An Invitation

WITH THIS BOOK of devotions you are invited on a forty-day spiritual journey in which you will explore the final day in the life of Jesus of Nazareth, beginning with the last meal he ate with his disciples and culminating in his death and burial. A postscript will invite you to consider the resurrection of Christ. I have written this book to be used during the season of Lent, though it can be used for any forty-day spiritual journey you might choose.

The Bible is filled with forty-day spiritual journeys in which people of faith have sought to hear from God. Elijah spent forty days fasting and seeking God at Mount Horeb. Moses fasted for forty days and forty nights at Mount Sinai when he received the Law. Noah watched the rain fall for forty days and forty nights as he sat in the ark pondering God's words to him. Jonah preached repentance to the people of Nineveh for forty days. And, most important of all, Jesus, before beginning his ministry, spent forty days and forty nights fasting in the wilderness while being tested by the devil.

Christians in the early 300s, if not before, began observing a period of fasting leading up to the celebration of Christ's resurrection which was (and still is in most of the world) known as *quadragesima* (Latin for "forty days" or "fortieth day"). In the English-speaking world we call this season Lent. It is a time of more intense spiritual seeking, devotion, and preparation climaxing in Holy Week with the crucifixion, burial, and resurrection of Jesus.

Each year during Lent, my wife, LaVon, reads through a classic devotional book focused on the suffering of Christ. It was her annual practice that led me to consider writing a forty-day devotional companion to my book *24 Hours That Changed the World.* In addition, LaVon traveled with me to the Holy Land as I was preparing the videos for the small-group study. She assisted in the filming. And together we retraced the footsteps of Jesus during the final hours of his life. In so many ways LaVon is the inspiration for this book. For this reason I dedicate it to her with love.

I have written this book of devotions and its companion book, *24 Hours That Changed the World,* so that you might devote forty days to listening as God speaks to you through the story of Jesus' final day, when he gave his life to redeem and save the human race from the brokenness and sin that have left us alienated from God and from one another.

This is the most tragic, moving, and powerful story ever told. My hope is that this small volume might help you hear and meditate upon this story and what it reveals about Jesus, about the Father he sought to serve, and about you.

Adam Hamilton

1. Preparing for the Meal

Then came the day of Unleavened Bread, on which the Passover lamb had to be sacrificed. So Jesus sent Peter and John, saying, "Go and prepare the Passover meal for us that we may eat it." They asked him, "Where do you want us to make preparations for it?" "Listen," he said to them, "when you have entered the city, a man carrying a jar of water will meet you; follow him into the house he enters and say to the owner of the house, 'The teacher asks you, "Where is the guest room, where I may eat the Passover with my disciples?"' He will show you a large room upstairs, already furnished. Make preparations for us there." So they went and found everything as he had told them; and they prepared the Passover meal.

(LUKE 22:7-13)

OUR JOURNEY WITH Jesus during his final twenty-four hours begins with a meal, or more precisely, with the preparations for a meal. Jesus sent John and Peter into Jerusalem to prepare the Passover Seder for the disciples. This entailed grocery shopping, making a sacrifice in the Temple, cooking, and setting the table. In their day this was the work of women or of servants.

I wonder how Peter and John felt about being asked to do this mundane work while Mary, Martha, and the other disciples remained with Jesus for the day.

I once met an executive who wanted to be used by God for a great purpose. He was a bit put out when the pastor suggested he begin by working anonymously in the kitchen of the homeless shelter preparing sandwiches on Saturdays. He felt he had far more potential than that— after all, he ran a large company and had leadership gifts. Realizing it was bad form to say no to the pastor's request, he began to prepare meals in the shelter.

But an interesting thing happened to him as he served each week: The act of serving began to change him—to diminish the pride that had crept into his heart and to cultivate compassion and humility. He began to have a vision of the needs of homeless people. Over time he invited friends and families to support the mission. He got his employees involved. Years later he was pivotal in developing a new facility that would better meet the needs of the homeless population. But all of this started with a request that he perform a task that, at first glance, he felt was beneath him.

Why did Jesus choose Peter and John for this task? What role would they play in the church after Jesus' death?

There is an unnamed disciple in this story. He owned a house large enough to have a second-floor guest room that could accommodate at least thirteen for supper. He was a man of some means; nevertheless he gladly played the part of a servant and freely gave of what he had, simply because Jesus asked. His guest room was likely the place the disciples hid following the Crucifixion and was perhaps even the place the 120 gathered on the Day of Pentecost, when the Spirit was poured out on the believers. If this is so, the man not only gave freely to the work of Jesus without ever being named, he did so at some personal cost. In what ways would you wish to be like this unnamed disciple?

Only in hindsight would Peter and John see the importance of the meal they prepared.

Lord, I offer myself to you. Use me to do whatever is needed, no matter how small. Like the unnamed disciple in the story, help me to serve without recognition. Amen.

2. Supper With Jesus

When the hour came, he took his place at the table, and the apostles with him. He said to them, "I have eagerly desired to eat this Passover with you before I suffer; for I tell you, I will not eat it until it is fulfilled in the kingdom of God." Then he took a cup, and after giving thanks he said, "Take this and divide it among yourselves; for I tell you that from now on I will not drink of the fruit of the vine until the kingdom of God comes." Then he took a loaf of bread, and when he had given thanks, he broke it and gave it to them, saying, "This is my body, which is given for you. Do this in remembrance of me." And he did the same with the cup after supper, saying, "This cup that is poured out for you is the new covenant in my blood." (LUKE 22:14-20)

IT IS SURPRISING how many of the Gospel stories of Jesus' ministry take place around a supper table. Luke's Gospel alone records eight such meals. At some of those meals we find Jesus eating with sinners and tax collectors. He ate in the homes of Pharisees. He was anointed by a prostitute at a meal and by a woman grateful to receive her brother back from the dead. He fed the multitudes with a few loaves and fish. After his resurrection he broke bread with two disciples in Emmaus and later ate fish with his disciples on the shore of Galilee.

But no meal is of more importance in the story of Jesus, or for Christians today, than the meal he ate after sunset the evening before he died. John's Gospel devotes five chapters to describing what Jesus said and did at that meal. Each of the Gospels tells this story, as does Paul in his first epistle to the Corinthians.

Jesus commanded his disciples to eat that meal and, as they did, to remember him. They were to see their eating of the bread and wine as a kind of participation in his sacrifice and as a tangible way of inviting him into their lives. (In 1 Corinthians 10, Paul calls it a *koinonia*—a sharing or fellowship with the body and blood of Jesus.) A man in his early forties died after a long bout with cancer, leaving behind a wife and two children. There was a particular casserole that was his favorite meal. Once a week his wife would continue to prepare this meal. As she and the children ate, she would tell her children stories of their father; and they would recall their own memories of their dad. His chair sat empty at the table, and they remembered him in a way that made them feel close to him and that continued to shape their lives.

I wonder if this is not what Jesus had in mind when he said, "As often as you do this, remember me." We should remember him not only in a morsel of bread and sip of wine during worship, but every time we sit down to break bread. Here

I am reminded of the old tradition, now nearly forgotten, of setting an extra place at the supper table as a way of inviting the Lord to "be present at our table." How might you remember him at each supper you eat? Consider reading a passage from the Gospels at every supper and spend time talking about the passage.

Lord, help me to remember you every time I break bread. Be present at my table, Lord. Help me never to forget that you are the bread of life who alone satisfies the deepest longings of my soul. Amen.

3. The Measure of Greatness

A dispute also arose among them as to which one of them was to be regarded as the greatest. But he said to them, "The kings of the Gentiles lord it over them; and those in authority over them are called benefactors. But not so with you; rather the greatest among you must become like the youngest, and the leader like one who serves.

(LUKE 22:24-26)

During supper Jesus, knowing that the Father had given all things into his hands, and that he had come from God and was going to God, got up from the table, took off his outer robe, and tied a towel around himself. Then he poured water into a basin and began to wash the disciples' feet and to wipe them with the towel that was tied around him. (JOHN 13:2b-5)

I FIND STUDYING the disciples in the Gospels to be a hopeful exercise for struggling Christians like me. About the time I feel that I am hopelessly lost, I read a passage such as Luke's account of the Last Supper where, as Jesus was preparing for his crucifixion, the disciples were sitting at the Passover meal secretly arguing over "which one of them was to be regarded as the greatest" (Luke 22:24). After three years with Jesus, this is what they were arguing about?

It was sometime around the sixth grade that I encountered the idea of popularity. At my school there were certain kids who were considered to be "cool"— defined by some combination of their appearance, their parents' wealth, their self-confidence, and their sporting prowess. By high school the characteristics of greatness were expanded to include those students nearly universally recognized by the student body for their talents. At the same time there was a second tier of greatness, defined within particular groups. In the band it was the "first chair" kids. In sports it was the "starters." Among the anti-social kids it was the kid who could be the most anti-social.

We do not stop disputing which of us is considered the greatest when we reach adulthood. How does society generally define greatness today?

Jesus, knowing that the disciples were arguing about which of them was greatest, did something most surprising. He got up from the table; went to the door; and picked up the pitcher of water, towel, and basin that had been left there so the disciples could wash their feet as they entered the room. None of them, apparently, had washed their own feet; and certainly none had thought about offering to wash the feet of their fellow disciples, or even the feet of Jesus. Performing such a task, like the meal preparations Jesus had sent Peter and John to make earlier that day, was the responsibility of a servant; and they were not servants—they were disciples. To their great discomfort, Jesus sank to his knees and one by one washed their feet. To make sure they understood the meaning of his gesture, he said in essence, "This is what true greatness looks like."

By washing his disciples' feet, the Son of God assumed the most humble of roles. Then he called all who would follow him to strive for that kind of greatness: to live their lives as humble servants. Long before the business world discovered the concept of "servant leadership," Jesus was calling his followers to adopt that lifestyle. Would those who know you describe you as one who in humility seeks to serve others?

Lord, you know that, like the disciples, I yearn to be considered great by others. Grant me a servant's heart so that I may discover that true greatness is found in humility and service. Amen.

4. One of You Will Betray Me

And when they had taken their places and were eating, Jesus said, "Truly I tell you, one of you will betray me, one who is eating with me." (MARK 14:18)

ALL FOUR GOSPELS record Jesus' words at the Last Supper predicting his betrayal at the hands of a disciple. (We will consider the reasons for that betrayal in a subsequent devotional reading.) They also record Jesus' prediction that before the night was out, Peter would deny knowing him. On his way to the garden of Gethsemane, Jesus went on to predict that the remaining disciples would abandon him.

Have you ever been betrayed, abandoned, or disappointed by a friend? Years ago one of my daughters came home in tears because a friend had "stabbed her in the back." My daughter announced that she would never be the girl's friend again. I understood how she felt. We all have felt betrayed by a friend at some point in our lives. Sometimes the person is not a friend but a family member or a professional we trusted.

There are forms of betrayal that are so severe and so psychologically damaging that breaking off the relationship is appropriate and necessary for emotional healing to occur. But most often what is required is grace.

Some years ago I was disappointed in a friend who had shared with another person something I had told him in confidence. My initial reaction was to decide he could not be trusted and to put some distance between us. But, prompted I believe by the Spirit, I called to mind moments when I had broken confidence or otherwise disappointed friends. It was hard to be angry with my friend when I had been guilty of doing similar things in the past. So I spoke to him, sharing my concern and disappointment; and he apologized. Our friendship was restored, and we continue to be good friends to this day.

Jesus knew his disciples would betray him, and yet he displayed extraordinary grace toward them at the meal. Knowing that Judas had already agreed to hand him over to the priests, Jesus still included him in the meal. Some scholars believe Jesus placed him to his left in the position of honor at the supper table. Knowing that Peter would deny knowing him, Jesus washed Peter's feet. Knowing that all would abandon him, he called them his friends; prayed for them; and said to them, "This is my blood of the new covenant poured out for you and for many for the forgiveness of sins."

Have you ever played the part of Judas or Peter or the other ten disciples by betraying, denying, or abandoning Jesus through what you have done or failed to do?

As you journey with Jesus in the closing hours of his life, is there anyone who has betrayed, abandoned, or disappointed you that he may be calling you to forgive?

Lord, forgive me for the ways I have played the part of Judas or Peter through what I have done or failed to do. As you have shown me mercy, help me to be merciful toward those who have betrayed or disappointed me. Amen.

5. What Is Your Price?

Then one of the twelve, who was called Judas Iscariot, went to the chief priests and said, "What will you give me if I betray him to you?" They paid him thirty pieces of silver. And from that moment he began to look for an opportunity to betray him. (MATTHEW 26:14-16)

BEFORE ARRIVING AT the Last Supper, Judas had already agreed to betray Jesus. Jesus predicted his betrayal at the supper; and following the meal, he sent Judas away, saying, "Do quickly what you are going to do" (John 13:27). Within a few hours Judas would arrive leading guards dispatched by the priests to arrest Jesus.

Why did Judas betray Jesus? This is a question that believers have debated for nearly two thousand years.

Some have speculated that Judas was a Zealot who began following Jesus anticipating that he would lead an uprising against the Romans. When it became clear that this was not Jesus' plan, Judas, in disappointment, betrayed Jesus. Some have suggested that Judas, by his actions, hoped to force Jesus to rise up against the religious authorities and the Romans. Perhaps Judas, who already felt a bit at odds with the disciples, was offended when Jesus chastised him at a supper in Bethany during the last week of Jesus' life. In these scenarios, Judas' politics may have come before his faith, or perhaps Judas' disappointment or hurt led him to succumb to evil.

We likely will not know the full motives of Judas' heart, but the Gospels do tell us that among his motives was a desire for money. John reports that Judas, as keeper of the money used in the ministry of Jesus, would occasionally steal from those funds (John 12:4-6). Matthew tells us that

Judas approached the chief priests asking, "What will you give me if I betray him to you?" (Matthew 26:15). They paid him thirty pieces of silver— about five weeks' wages for an average worker.

Money has a strange way of affecting us. Paul tells us that "the love of money is a root of all kinds of evil" (1 Timothy 6:10). Jesus was tempted with riches by the devil and regularly preached about the struggle human beings have with a desire for wealth. That struggle is still with us today, as shown by the human greed and gluttony behind the economic crisis that began in 2008.

On several occasions Jesus spoke to people struggling with greed. He told the man we call "the rich young ruler" that the only way he could break free of his love of possessions was to part with them all by giving everything away to the poor. On another occasion he told a man struggling with greed, "One's life does not consist in the abundance of possessions"

(Luke 12:15). I have committed these words to memory and frequently repeat them, as I am regularly tempted to focus on acquisition. Eventually, the love of money can and will come into conflict with our love of God. In Judas' case, the love of money won out. Slowly and by degrees, he came to rationalize his taking from the common purse and ultimately his betrayal of Jesus. Do you ever find your faith in conflict with your finances? Are you willing to give as God calls you to? Are you completely honest in your business dealings? on your tax return? Do you ever compromise your values in order to make the sale, close the deal, or get the raise?

Lord, forgive me for the times I have compromised my faith for the sake of having more. Help me to remember that my life "does not consist in the abundance of [my] possessions" and to desire to serve you with all that I am and all that I have. Amen.

6. I Go to Prepare a Place for You

Do not let your hearts be troubled. Believe in God, believe also in me. In my Father's house there are many dwelling places. If it were not so, would I have told you that I go to prepare a place for you? And if I go and prepare a place for you, I will come again and will take you to myself, so that where I am, there you may be also.

(JOHN 14:1-3)

IN THE LAST twenty years as a pastor, I have sat with many people as they approached their own deaths—at home, in the hospital, in nursing homes, at the local hospice house.

I remember sitting with one such man on his back porch on a beautiful fall day. He was a man my age nearing the end of his battle with ALS (often referred to as Lou Gehrig's Disease).

We spoke about his young boys and how he had recorded video messages for them to watch when they grew up. He described what he wanted for his funeral. And we discussed what Christians believe about the afterlife. Then we prayed, entrusting his life to God's care.

On the evening of the Last Supper, Jesus spoke with his disciples as a man preparing for his own death. He had much to tell them. The future of his mission would rest in their hands, and he sought to prepare them for what lay ahead. They would see his death, and later they would face hardship and persecution of their own.

John gives us the most complete account of what Jesus said that night; he devoted five of his Gospel's twenty-one chapters to what Jesus said and did on that occasion. John's account of Jesus' words at the Last Supper includes some of the most loved of all Gospel passages. Here Jesus promised that he would not leave the disciples alone but would send them the *paraklete* ("comforter" or "counselor"), that is, the Holy Spirit. He called them to "abide" in him as a branch abides in a vine and draws sustenance from it. He commanded them to "love one another." Undoubtedly the best-loved of his words that night are found in John 14: "Do not let your hearts be troubled. Believe in God, believe also in me. In my Father's house there are many dwelling places. If it were not so, would I have told you that I go to prepare a place for you? And if I go and prepare a place for you, I will come again and will take you to myself, so that where I am, there you may be also" (John 14:1-3).

I have read those words many times to people who faced death, and the words have brought comfort. When speaking of trusting Christ, I tell the story of my children who, when they were small, would climb three or four steps up the stairwell in our house and shout to me, "Daddy, Daddy, come play flying squirrel!" I would then stand at the bottom of the stairwell; and they would throw themselves off the steps headfirst into my arms, squealing and giggling and shouting for joy. The floor was ceramic tile, and had they fallen they would have been hurt; but they were never afraid because they knew their daddy was strong enough to catch them, and he loved them so much he would not let them fall. Many times I have told those who were dying that this is what trust looks like. I have invited them to close their eyes and imagine resting in God's arms, trusting that he is strong enough to protect them and that he loves them so much he would never let them go.

Jesus promised, as he was preparing for his own death, that he would prepare a place for us that we might one day be with him.

> *Lord, help me to trust that you love me; that you will not let go of me; and that you have prepared a place for me to be with you in your eternal kingdom when my earthly life is over. Amen.*

7. The Mandates
of Maundy Thursday

I am the vine, you are the branches. Those who abide in me and I in them bear much fruit My Father is glorified by this, that you bear much fruit and become my disciples. As the Father has loved me, so I have loved you; abide in my love. If you keep my commandments, you will abide in my love, just as I have kept my Father's commandments and abide in his love. I have said these things to you so that my joy may be in you, and that your joy may be complete.

This is my commandment, that you love one another as I have loved you. No one has greater love than this, to lay down one's life for one's friends. (JOHN 15:5, 8-13)

THE THURSDAY OF the Last Supper is often called Maundy Thursday. The name, it is thought, comes from the Latin word *mandatum*, which means "commandment." On that night Jesus gave several commandments to his disciples.

He commanded them to remember him by means of a meal of bread and wine ("Do this in remembrance of me" [Luke 22:19].). As he washed their feet, he commanded them to follow his example by serving one another. And in John 15 we read that he commanded them to "abide in me" and to "love one another." It is the command to abide in Christ that we consider today.

As Jesus prepared to leave his disciples, he called them to "abide in me." Jesus used the metaphor of a grapevine and its branches to describe what he was asking of them—and of us. We are to remain connected to Jesus even if we cannot physically see him. We are to draw strength and spiritual nourishment from our relationship with him. We are to do this through prayer, meditation, worship, and the study of his life and teachings as found in the Scripture and through talking about him with others. Your reading of this book is an attempt on your part to abide in him by reflecting upon his final hours on Earth.

A man I know had at one time had a vibrant spiritual life. He had felt God's presence in his life; had been excited about serving God and others; and had always been looking for ways to bless, care for, and encourage others. When I looked at him, I saw joy. But something happened to him a couple of years ago. He dropped out of church—not all at once, but slowly. He missed a Sunday here and there. Soon he was absent more often than he was present for worship. He stopped attending his small group. He stopped serving others. He stopped reading his Bible. He stopped giving his tithes. And eventually, he stopped praying. I saw him the other day. The joy I had once seen in his eyes was gone, and he recently had made some decisions that would have continuing tragic consequences. His actions had produced in him no small amount of anxiety. Gone was the fruit I had once seen in his life. This is what can happen when we become disconnected from the Vine.

If we remain connected to the Vine, pursuing practices that help us abide in Christ, we will bear fruit—not just praying, reading the Bible, worshiping, and giving, but demonstrating our love for others through our actions. This love is more than just warm affection; it is a willingness to put others before ourselves and to practice kindness, to do justice, to seek the good of others, and to bless.

Are you bearing fruit? Would others describe you as a loving person? Why, or why not?

> *Jesus, help me to abide in you—to speak with you, listen for your voice, worship you, and study your words. Please help me to live a life of love toward others. Amen.*

8. A Song of Praise in the Face of Death

When they had sung the hymn, they went out to the Mount of Olives. (MARK 14:26)

THE LAST SUPPER likely concluded sometime just before midnight. Jesus had broken bread with the disciples, washed their feet, predicted Judas' betrayal, and taught the disciples the final lessons he wanted them to learn before his death. Now he was preparing to lead them across the Kidron Valley to the garden of Gethsemane, where he knew he would be arrested. The end was drawing near. Yet there was one last thing he and his disciples did at the supper before beginning the journey to Gethsemane: They sang a hymn together.

The hymn that traditionally closes the Passover Seder, and hence the hymn that Mark likely refers to in this passage, is Psalm 118. This hymn begins and ends with the words "O Give thanks to the LORD, for he is good; / his steadfast love endures forever!" (Psalm 118:1, 29). The psalm is an invitation to trust in God even in the face of enemies that would destroy. With the singing of these words, Jesus prepared himself and his disciples for what lay ahead.

Singing praise to God in the face of adversity is an act of defiance toward evil. It is also an act of trust in God, one that gives strength, peace, and hope. By singing praise to God in the face of hardship or even death, we are saying, "No matter what happens, no matter how bad things may be, I will trust in God to deliver me." As Jesus approached his death, he sang a hymn of praise to God.

The apostles followed this practice. In Acts 16 we read that Paul and Silas had been flogged by the authorities in Philippi and then cast into a dungeon, their feet in shackles. But Acts records, "About midnight Paul and Silas were praying and singing hymns to God" from their prison cell as the other prisoners listened (Acts 16:25). In 1 Thessalonians 5:16-18, Paul instructs us to "rejoice always, pray without ceasing, give thanks in all circumstances."

Jay was a man about my age, and he had been battling cancer. He had been released from the hospital recently, and it was becoming clear that the treatment would not be successful. Because he was weak from both the cancer and the treatment, I was utterly astounded when I saw Jay walk into worship on Sunday morning. It was Easter, and

Jay was not going to miss Easter worship. That was the last time he came to church. Several weeks later, he died. But I will never forget the image of Jay singing, praising God, and being surrounded by his church family on that day.

As Jesus approached his own death, he sang a hymn with his disciples. Take a moment to read the words of the hymn Jesus probably sang that night, and then reflect on what those words would have meant to Jesus at that time. Read Psalm 118.

> *Lord, I give thanks to you; for you are good, and your love endures forever. Help me, even in the face of adversity, to sing your praise and to trust in you. Amen.*

9. The Mount of Olives

He came out and went, as was his custom, to the Mount of Olives; and the disciples followed him. (LUKE 22:39)

WHY DID JESUS return to the Mount of Olives to pray and await his arrest?

The upper room where he ate the Last Supper was just a stone's throw from the high priest's home where he would be brought after his arrest to stand trial before the Sanhedrin. The garden of Gethsemane on the Mount of Olives, by contrast, was a twenty- to twenty-five-minute walk from the high priest's home. Following his arrest in the garden of Gethsemane, Jesus would be led in chains back down into the valley and then up Mount Zion to stand trial. I recently walked that path, and I can tell you that the journey is strenuous and left me winded. I cannot imagine doing it in chains. Why didn't Jesus, knowing his arrest was imminent, remain in the upper room in prayer awaiting Judas and the Temple guard?

Luke tells us that it was Jesus' custom to go to the Mount of Olives each day during the last week of his life. John tells us that Jesus often met on the Mount of Olives with his disciples. This place had special meaning for Jesus. But why?

The prophet Zechariah holds the clue. Starting with his entrance into Jerusalem from the Mount of Olives a few days earlier, it is clear that Jesus had been reflecting on the words of this prophet. It was Zechariah who had described Judah's king riding on a donkey. In Zechariah 14:4 we read, "On that day his feet shall stand on the Mount of Olives"; and Zechariah continued in verse 9, "And the LORD will become king over all the earth; on that day the LORD will be one and his name one."

At Jesus' birth, the shepherds and wise men came to see him who was born king of the Jews. When Jesus began his public ministry, he told parables of the Kingdom and did deeds of power demonstrating the nature of the Kingdom. He taught people to pray, "Thy Kingdom come, thy will be done, on earth as it is in heaven."

In a few hours a crown of thorns would be placed on his brow and a sign nailed over his head: "This is Jesus, the King of the Jews" (Matthew 27:37).

Jesus had come to the Mount of Olives in part because there he felt closely connected to the mission his Father had sent him to fulfill. But he had also come so his presence and arrest on the Mount of Olives would be one more sign of his true identity and one more picture of the blindness of those who sought his death.

Jesus said, "The kingdom of God is among you" (Luke 17:21). It is in yielding our hearts and lives to God's will that we become a part of his kingdom. Take a moment today to yield your heart and life to God, to seek to do his will in your life.

> *God, I accept you as my King. Help me to know and do your will. May my life bring glory to your name. Amen.*

10. He Began to Be Distressed and Agitated

They went to a place called Gethsemane; and he said to his disciples, "Sit here while I pray." He took with him Peter and James and John, and began to be distressed and agitated. And he said to them, "I am deeply grieved, even to death; remain here, and keep awake."

(MARK 14:32-34)

IT IS DIFFICULT to picture Jesus "distressed and agitated." Somehow it seems out of character. Angry, I can see. But agitated? sorrowful? afraid? Yet the Gospels clearly portray Jesus as being in deep anguish on this occasion. He threw himself on the ground in prayer. He perspired drops of blood. Why?

Some feel the need to spiritualize Jesus' agony in the garden, but to do so misses the point. The Gospel writers were not afraid to tell us that Jesus was feeling distressed about his impending arrest, torture, and crucifixion. His distress did not diminish him in their eyes. Jesus was feeling what a human being should feel when facing what he faced. This is part of the power of the Incarnation. In Jesus Christ, God experienced anguish, sorrow, and suffering as human beings do.

In our church we have a number of support groups for people, including those diagnosed with cancer, those with loved ones suffering from mental illness, those who have lost a spouse, and those who have endured the death of a child. I can sit in on these groups and seek to empathize. But for participants, the real power of the groups comes from being with others who have walked in their shoes.

The writer of the Epistle to the Hebrews called Jesus our "high priest" who goes to the Father on our behalf. I believe the writer had the agony in the garden in mind when he wrote, "For we do not have a high priest who is unable to sympathize with our weaknesses, but we have one who in every respect has been tested as we are, yet without sin. Let us therefore approach the throne of grace with boldness, so that we may receive mercy and find grace to help in time of need" (Hebrews 4:15-16).

I am grateful to the Gospel writers for telling us that Jesus knew what it was to be agitated, sorrowful, overwhelmed, and afraid. When I am feeling these things, I remember Jesus' agony in the garden. And as I pray to him, I know that the one I am talking to has walked in my shoes; understands me in my moments of despair; and intercedes, as a high priest, on my behalf.

*Lord, you know what it is like to feel over-
whelmed with sorrow and grief and to be
anxious about the path that lies ahead. In my
times of agony and fear, hold me close. In my
doubt and despair, draw me near. Help me in
my time of need. Amen.*

11. Father, Let This Cup Pass From Me

And going a little farther, he threw himself on the ground and prayed that, if it were possible, the hour might pass from him. He said, "Abba, Father, for you all things are possible; remove this cup from me." (MARK 14:35-36)

AT THE GARDEN of Gethsemane in Jerusalem stands the Church of All Nations, also known as the Basilica of the Agony. It was built in the early 1900s atop the ruins of two previous churches, one dating to the time of the crusaders and the earliest dating back to the fourth century. The Church of All Nations is, for many, one of the most moving places to pray in the Holy Land. In front of the altar is what remains of a limestone rock outcropping that tradition says was the place where Jesus came to pray.

Stars adorn the ceiling of the dimly lit church, taking worshipers back to the night when Christ prayed in this place. Pilgrims are invited to kneel around the exposed bedrock, touching it while praying as Jesus did nearly two thousand years ago.

Somewhere near this place Jesus threw himself to the ground on that night and prayed, "Abba, Father, for you all things are possible; remove this cup from me" (Mark 14:36). In essence he was praying, "Father, please find another way to accomplish your plans—a way that does not involve the rejection of the priests, the cries of the crowd, the torture of the soldiers, the humiliation and pain of the cross, and the darkness of death."

On this night Jesus resisted the path that was laid out before him. He struggled with what he believed was God's will. He was not the first to have struggled in this way. Read Exodus 4, where you will find Moses giving God excuses as to why he could not return to Egypt to confront Pharaoh. Or consider the story of Jonah, who refused God's command and only obeyed after three days of soaking in a great fish's gastric juices.

Have you ever found yourself struggling with God? Was there a path God would have you take that you wanted to avoid? Was there a risk that seemed too great or a price that seemed too high? Have you ever prayed with Moses, "Lord, send someone else"? Have you ever run with Jonah in the direction opposite where God was calling you to go? Have you ever knelt with Jesus in the garden, saying, "Remove this cup from me"?

Pursuing God's will is at times costly. Jesus said, "If any want to become my followers, let them deny themselves and take up their cross and follow me" (Matthew 16:24). Are you willing, even grudgingly, to go where God calls and do what God asks, regardless of the cost? After arguing with the Lord, Moses relented and returned to Egypt, risking death to lead the Israelites to freedom. Jonah, in the darkness of the great fish's belly, finally said, "OK, send me!" And Jesus, despite praying for the cup to pass from him, accepted it when Judas handed it to him and drank from it, laying down his life for God's mission.

Recently, I visited the Basilica of the Agony, touching the stone before the altar where Jesus may have prayed. I was reminded of times past when a cup far less difficult and deadly was passed to me, and I refused to drink. Kneeling there, I tried to feel his agony. And I thanked him for the costliness of his grace.

Lord, you understand my weakness and fear. You know the times I refused the cup you passed to me. Forgive me, I pray. Help me to say yes when you call me to pursue your mission for my life, no matter what the cost. Amen.

12. Two Gardens

There was a garden, which he and his disciples entered.
(JOHN 18:1)

Not what I want, but what you want. (MARK 14:36)

JOHN'S GOSPEL BEGINS with these words:
"In the beginning…" John chose these particular words as a way of pointing to the meaning
of the gospel. With them he intended to take us
back to Genesis.

The story of Adam and Eve serves as the back-
drop of John's Gospel. Adam and Eve were given
a garden in which to live. God planted the garden
and then called them to tend it. There, before a
tree, they were tested and tempted. They suc-
cumbed to the tempter, turned from God's way;

and Paradise was lost. Their story is, of course, our story. Each of us has known the will of God; but at some time, at some level, we have turned away from it. We have eaten the forbidden fruit.

John alone tells us that the place where Jesus prayed on the night he was arrested was a garden. Matthew and Mark do not tell us this; they only tell us it was the place of the oil press. (This is the meaning of the word *Gethsemane*.) The Gospel of Luke tells us that Jesus prayed on the Mount of Olives but is no more specific. John alone tells us that Jesus went to a garden to pray.

In this garden Eden was being reversed. Jesus' public ministry began with the temptation to lay aside God's will and to accept all the riches of the world from the hands of the devil. And now here, at the end of his life, Jesus was in a garden, facing the temptation to save himself and flee. I wonder what the serpent whispered to him that night: "Did God really intend for you to suffer and die?" Or, "Surely you don't believe that if you die, anything will change." Or, "What good will you be when you are dead?"

Or, "Do you really believe that this band of misfits you call disciples can carry on your mission? Look at them— they're sleeping! It's not too late, Jesus. Run!"

Two gardens. In one, Adam and Eve were warned that death would come if they disobeyed; and they still could not resist the forbidden fruit. In the other, Jesus was told he could avoid death if he would only disobey. How different were the responses to temptation between the first Adam and Jesus (whom Paul calls the "second Adam"). In the first garden Adam prayed, "Not thy will, but *mine* be done"; and Paradise was lost. In the second garden, as the disciples slept and the Temple guard made their way across the Kidron Valley, Jesus prayed, "Not my will, but *thine* be done." His prayer was central to the restoration of what had been lost in Eden.

John Wesley, the founder of Methodism, popularized the following prayer, meant to help those who use it to follow in Jesus' steps, surrendering to the will of God:

I am no longer my own, but thine. Put me to what you will. Rank me with whom you will. Put me to doing; put me to suffering. Let me be employed for thee or laid aside for thee, exalted for thee or brought low for thee. Let me be full. Or let me be empty. Let me have all things. Or let me have nothing. I freely and heartily yield all things to thy pleasure and disposal. Amen.

13. He Came and Found Them Sleeping

He came and found them sleeping; and he said to Peter, "Simon, are you asleep? Could you not keep awake one hour? Keep awake and pray that you may not come into the time of trial; the spirit indeed is willing, but the flesh is weak." And again he went away and prayed, saying the same words. And once more he came and found them sleeping, for their eyes were very heavy; and they did not know what to say to him. He came a third time and said to them, "Are you still sleeping and taking your rest? Enough! The hour has come." (MARK 14:37-41)

NEAR GETHSEMANE THERE is a cave where some believe the disciples were told to wait while Jesus went into the olive grove to pray late that night. Perhaps he did not want them to see him in his greatest distress. But before

going into the garden, Jesus asked his three clos-
est companions, Peter, James, and John, to go
with him. He revealed to the three of them just
how deeply grieved he was. He asked them to
"stay awake with me" (Matthew 26:38) and then
asked them to remain in the garden as he went
just a little farther to pray by himself.

Jesus fell to the ground to pray; but then,
after a period of time, he went back to Peter,
James, and John. He repeated this pattern—praying alone and then returning to the disciples—
three times before Judas arrived with the Temple
guard to arrest him. Some have suggested a par-
allel between these three occasions and the three
temptations Jesus experienced at the beginning
of his ministry. The fact that the disciples had
fallen asleep each time points to their own temptation and, more importantly, to the temptation
of his followers ever since to sleep when Christ
most needs us.

At times as a pastor I have been "asleep on the job." On the day I was writing this devotion, a member of my church died, someone about whom I truly cared. I knew that he was ill. I had spoken with his wife earlier in the year. I pastor a very large church with a team of pastors and laypeople who provide care for our members, and he was cared for by others in that group. However, when I received notice about his death, I was stunned and grieved. I called his wife to convey my condolences. But I felt such sadness that I had missed the chance to be with him in the days leading up to his death. I had been asleep on the job.

In the New Testament, "being awake" is a phrase used to describe being spiritually ready, most often for the return of Christ, but also ready to do what the Lord needs whenever he needs us. It entails a watchfulness and a way of paying attention to what is happening around us, to the needs of others, and to the direction of the

Holy Spirit. We are meant to stay awake and keep watch.

Have you ever, like me, and like those first disciples, fallen asleep when Christ truly needed you?

> *Lord, many times my spirit has been willing to do your will; but my flesh has been weak. Help me to stay awake— to listen for your voice and to be used by you to care for your people. Amen.*

14. Betrayed With a Kiss

Immediately, while he was still speaking, Judas, one of the twelve, arrived; and with him there was a crowd with swords and clubs, from the chief priests, the scribes, and the elders. Now the betrayer had given them a sign, saying, "The one I will kiss is the man; arrest him and lead him away under guard." So when he came, he went up to him at once and said, "Rabbi!" and kissed him. Then they laid hands on him and arrested him.

(MARK 14:43-46)

BY NOW IT WAS well after midnight. The Temple guards, brandishing swords and clubs and carrying torches, would have been heard and seen from a distance. Jesus awoke Peter, James, and John one last time. The other disciples came running; yet they hung back among the trees, uncertain what was happening.

Seeing the guards, they were stunned to see one of their own leading the pack.

This brings us to Judas. Another tragic character in this story, he clearly was conflicted. Upon giving Jesus up to the guards, he needed only to have pointed out Jesus and said, "He's that one, there!" Instead he told the guard, "The one I will kiss is the man" (Matthew 26:48; Mark 14:44). Was the kiss an attempt to rub salt in the wound of his betrayal? Or was it an expression of his conflicted feelings about Jesus, feelings that later in the day would lead to Judas' suicide?

I know a young man who grew up in the church, attending Sunday school every week and vacation Bible school every year. He was involved in youth group and went on mission trips and to summer camp. It appeared that the young man personally trusted Christ and had pledged to follow him. But for now he has turned away from Jesus. The lure of the world's pleasures, of what he believes is real freedom, has proved irresistible to him. When pressed, he will say that there may be a God and that Jesus was a good teacher; but he has a list of reasons why he does not follow Christ.

I have watched hundreds of young men and women take this path. Most of the people in the church I pastor have at one time turned away from Christ and the faith in which they were reared. But ultimately they returned, finding that they do love Christ and find in him "the way, the truth, and the life." I am confident that the young man I just described will one day find his way back to faith.

Perhaps more closely akin to Judas' actions is what happens in the lives of believers who gather for worship each week, expressing their love for Christ on Sunday but on Monday living in a way that indicates that they never knew him.

Judas betrayed Jesus with a kiss, a sign perhaps of the conflict that raged within him—of a love for this man and yet a desire to be free of him, of a love for God's kingdom and a desire for the kingdoms of this world.

What will you and I do with our conflicts?

Lord, you know the conflict that rages at times within me. I wish to love and follow you. I attend worship and praise you. Then I find myself struggling with the desires of this world or seeking the affirmation and praise of others, and through my words and deeds I betray you. Forgive me, I pray. Help me to follow you faithfully. Amen.

15. The Trial Before the Righteous

They took Jesus to the high priest; and all the chief priests, the elders, and the scribes were assembled. Now the chief priests and the whole council were looking for testimony against Jesus to put him to death. (MARK 14:53, 55)

JESUS WAS BOUND and led by the Temple guard across the Kidron Valley and up the fairly steep path on the eastern side of Mount Zion, to the palace of the high priest. This place served as both the residence of the high priest and an alternative gathering place for the Sanhedrin, the Jewish ruling council who typically met in the Chamber of the Hewn Stone at the Temple. Stone stairs still mark the last part of the path, stairs that Jesus may well have trod on that night.

The Church of Saint Peter in Gallicantu is built over what are said to be the ruins of the high priest's house. Descending a staircase to the lower level, one enters a chapel; and in the center of this chapel there is an opening in the floor that leads to a pit—a dungeon. It is thought that Jesus was lowered into this pit by ropes and was kept there until very early in the morning, when he was drawn back out of this dark place and brought before the council for trial on charges of blasphemy. Can you picture Jesus lying on the stone floor of this pit, awaiting his trial? Some suggest that he may have prayed the words of Psalm 88 as he lay there. (Take a moment and read Psalm 88 to see why they believe this.)

The members of the Sanhedrin sat in a semicircle for such trials. The accused stood before these seventy-one defenders of Jewish orthodoxy. Picture the tragic irony of this scene: God had taken on flesh to walk on the planet he had created, among the people he had called his own. He had healed the sick, opened the eyes of the blind, and loved sinners; but he was arrested by the religious leaders, unrecognized by them, and charged with blasphemy!

The story of the last twenty-four hours of Jesus' life is a case study in the human condition. At least five of the seven deadly sins were represented in the actions of the disciples, the religious leaders, the Roman authorities, and the crowd. Through those actions, the people indicted themselves and served to illustrate the premise of the story that was unfolding before their eyes: Humankind needed to be saved.

I recently spoke with a young woman who worked at a church. She had watched as her supervisor treated other staff members and volunteers poorly. She said to me, "Watching how religious people act is enough to make me question whether I want to be a Christian."

I empathized with her for a moment and then asked her this question: "Do you think you or I have ever done anything that might lead someone else to say the same thing about us?"

Most of us live at times in ways that are antithetical to our faith. We often are blind to our sin. And tragically we sometimes cloak our sin in the language of faith. We cite Scripture to justify our fears and bigotry. We behave judgmentally and call it righteousness.

Have you ever said or done something that you felt was God's will and only later realized that you had missed the mark?

Lord, help me never to use my faith as a cover for sin. Forgive me for the times when I have, in the name of my faith, acted in ways that betrayed you. Amen.

16. Destroy This Temple

Many gave false testimony against him, and their testimony did not agree. Some stood up and gave false testimony against him, saying, "We heard him say, 'I will destroy this temple that is made with hands, and in three days I will build another, not made with hands.'" But even on this point their testimony did not agree.

(MARK 14:56-59)

EARLY IN THE MORNING, the trial of Jesus before the Sanhedrin finally began. Jewish law required two to three witnesses in order to convict someone of a capital offense (Deuteronomy 19:15-21). Witnesses were brought before the accused, one at a time, and gave their testimony to the Sanhedrin.

Who were these witnesses, and why did they testify against Jesus? It is likely that some were among the moneychangers and merchants Jesus had driven out of the Temple only days before. Matthew indicates that there was no shortage of people willing to say things disparaging of Jesus, but either the accusations did not rise to the level of a capital crime or the testimonies did not agree. The only accusation on which two witnesses agreed was that Jesus had said, "I am able to destroy the temple of God and to build it in three days" (Matthew 26:61).

The Temple was of tremendous importance to the Jewish people. Threatening to destroy it would be an act of terrorism and blasphemy. The Temple represented God's presence among his people. The Holy of Holies was God's throne room and the ark of the covenant his throne. The Temple was destroyed for the last time in AD 70, but to this day Jews gather to pray at the Western Wall—the foundation wall that remains from the Temple. Threatening to destroy the Temple would be a crime punishable by death.

Yet the witnesses had misquoted Jesus. His actual words, according to John, were "[You] destroy this temple, and in three days I will raise it up" (John 2:19). John goes on to tell us that when Jesus spoke these words, he was referring not to the temple Herod had built, but to Jesus' own body.

Once again we see the irony in this story. Solomon, in dedicating the Temple, had recognized that God does not live in buildings made by human hands. In Jesus, God had come to live among his people. The glory of the Lord had come in human flesh. When Jesus walked into the Temple courts, the glory of the Lord entered that place. But the merchants, the moneychangers, and the priests could not see it. And these men who were accusing Jesus of threatening to destroy the earthly Temple were themselves preparing to destroy Jesus, the temple of the Lord—in other words, to do the very thing they were accusing him of doing.

After the death, resurrection, and ascension of Jesus, the early church leaders taught that the temple of God was no longer the building in Jerusalem but the church itself and even each individual believer. They taught that the Holy Spirit dwells in us and that wherever God's people gather for worship, the Spirit is present in the midst of them. Filled with the Spirit, we are meant to represent God's presence and reality in the world.

Lord, fill me anew with your Holy Spirit. Make me a living temple, that in me others might see you. Amen.

17. Blasphemy

The high priest asked him, "Are you the Messiah, the Son of the Blessed One?" Jesus said, "I am; and

> *'you will see the Son of Man*
> *seated at the right hand of the Power,'*
> *and 'coming with the clouds of heaven.' "*

Then the high priest tore his clothes and said, "Why do we still need witnesses? You have heard his blasphemy! What is your decision?" All of them condemned him as deserving death. Some began to spit on him, to blindfold him, and to strike him, saying to him, "Prophesy!" The guards also took him over and beat him.

(MARK 14:61b-65)

A LL WEEK THE PRIESTS had waited to hear Jesus claim to be the Messiah. He had done everything but publicly say the words. He would reveal this, but in his own time. Now was the time.

When the high priest asked, "Are you the Messiah?" Jesus responded with three allusions to the Hebrew Bible that every member of the Sanhedrin would recognize. His most direct response, "I am," was itself a veiled reference identifying himself with God. In Exodus 3:14 when Moses asked God by what name God should be addressed, God said, "I AM." With this name God was stating that he was the very source and essence of being and of life. Paul captured this point in his speech in Athens when he quoted the Greek poet: "In him we live and move and have our being" (Acts 17:28). In John 8:58 we read that Jesus had said, "Before Abraham was, I am"; and as a result the people had tried to stone him to death. In the event that the Sanhedrin did not understand his first allusion, Jesus made his second allusion even plainer. It was a quote from Daniel 7:13-14:

> *I saw one like a human being [son of man]*
> *coming with the clouds of heaven....*

> *To him was given dominion*
> *and glory and kingship,*
> *that all peoples, nations, and languages*
> *should serve him.*
> *His dominion is an everlasting dominion*
> *that shall not pass away,*
> *and his kingship is one*
> *that shall never be destroyed.*

For the high priest and the Sanhedrin, Jesus' identification with Daniel's words represented a second act of blasphemy.

Then Jesus told the Sanhedrin that they would see him at the right hand of God. This third and final allusion was to Psalm 110:1, originally a psalm of David, which promised that the king would sit at the right hand of God and that God would make the king's enemies his footstool. This allusion would not have been lost on the Sanhedrin as they were seeking Jesus' demise.

After hearing Jesus' words, the high priest tore his clothes; and the entire Sanhedrin pronounced

Jesus guilty of blasphemy and condemned him to die. They blindfolded him, spat upon him, and beat him. In doing so, were they motivated by fear, or hate, or both? Whatever their motives, the members of the council had revealed their true nature: There was darkness beneath the surface of their piety and devotion.

> *Lord, it is easy for me, like the Sanhedrin members, to act in ways that seem religious while sin lurks in my heart. Forgive me and change me from the inside out. I trust you as the source of life and hail you as my King. Ready me for the day of your return. Amen.*

18. Giving Peter Credit

Then they seized him and led him away, bringing him into the high priest's house. But Peter was following at a distance. When they had kindled a fire in the middle of the courtyard and sat down together, Peter sat among them. (LUKE 22:54-55)

MUCH EMPHASIS HAS been given to Peter's denial of Jesus on the night of Jesus' arrest. We will consider this in the next reading. But before considering Peter's failure of nerve, let's look at the acts of courage that preceded his denial.

After the Last Supper, Jesus had predicted that the disciples would all desert him. Peter replied, "Even though all become deserters, I will not"; and "Even though I must die with you, I will not deny you" (Mark 14:29, 31).

Can you feel Peter's earnest desire to stand with Jesus no matter what the cost?

When Judas arrived with the Temple guard and the guard went to seize Jesus, John tells us it was Peter who drew his sword and cut off the ear of the high priest's servant. Peter may not have been a good aim with his sword (or perhaps he was only aiming for the ear), but he appears to have been willing to stand by his words and to die defending Jesus.

After Jesus was seized, the other disciples fled. Peter alone followed the guards, though at a distance so as not to be captured. Finally, when Jesus was taken into the high priest's house, Peter actually dared to enter the courtyard where many of those who had seized Jesus were standing.

These are hardly the acts of a coward.

I stood with a woman as we prepared to board an airplane for southern Africa. She had never left the United States and now was going to spend two weeks in the slums of Johannesburg and Durban, South Africa, and among the bush people of northern Zambia. The news had recently described violence in some of the areas she would be visiting. She would face the risk of catching malaria and would be visiting and ministering to women who were dying of AIDS. Yet there she stood, preparing to board the plane, showing only a hint of the anxiety she must have been feeling. In her own way, she too was exhibiting courage.

It took remarkable courage for Peter to enter the courtyard that night. When has your faith required courage of you?

Lord, grant me courage to follow you even when it is frightening. Amen.

19. A Failure of Nerve

One of the servant-girls of the high priest came by. When she saw Peter warming himself, she stared at him and said, "You also were with Jesus, the man from Nazareth." But he denied it, saying, "I do not know or understand what you are talking about." And he went out into the forecourt. Then the cock crowed. And the servant-girl, on seeing him, began again to say to the bystanders, "This man is one of them." But again he denied it. Then after a little while the bystanders again said to Peter, "Certainly you are one of them; for you are a Galilean." But he began to curse, and he swore an oath, "I do not know this man you are talking about." At that moment the cock crowed for the second time. Then Peter... broke down and wept. (MARK 14:66-72)

AS JESUS WENT ON TRIAL before the Sanhedrin, Peter stood in the courtyard of the high priest. He was surrounded by people who were willing to testify against Jesus in the trial and who had aided in his arrest. Three times Peter was confronted and asked whether he was a follower of Jesus. Three times he denied it.

Have you ever faced a moment when you were afraid to be identified as a follower of Jesus? It is likely, if you have, that the stakes were much lower for you than they were for Peter. Perhaps you were unwilling to say your mealtime blessing because you were eating with others whom you feared might think less of you. Perhaps you joined in a conversation or activity in order to fit in rather than standing up and being counted as a Christ-follower. In a split second you, like Peter, may have decided to hide your identity as a Christian.

There are at least three things to note in the story of Peter's denial: First, Peter could have left the courtyard after the servant girl accused him of being a follower of Jesus. While it is true that he denied Jesus, he did not leave the courtyard. Why? Because he still loved Jesus. Second, we should note the way Peter's denial affected him: He was deeply grieved by what he had done, and he wept bitterly. Third, this story is told in all four Gospels despite the fact that it would have been deeply embarrassing to Peter, the prince of the apostles. Why did all four Gospel writers feel comfortable telling the story? I believe it was because Peter had told it again and again across the Roman Empire. Telling the story could have been his way of saying, "I denied knowing the Lord, but after his resurrection he took me back and restored me; and by his grace I am what I am today!"

This is a story of fear and denial. But it is also a story of grace and restoration. If the Lord could restore Peter, surely he can do it for us, despite the many ways we have denied him by our words and actions.

> *Lord, there have been moments when I, like Peter, have been torn between my desire for the acceptance of others and my desire to please you. Forgive me and help me boldly stand and be counted as one of your followers. Amen.*

20. If Judas Had Only Waited

When Judas, his betrayer, saw that Jesus was condemned, he repented and brought back the thirty pieces of silver to the chief priests and the elders. He said, "I have sinned by betraying innocent blood." But they said, "What is that to us? See to it yourself." Throwing down the pieces of silver in the temple, he departed; and he went and hanged himself. (MATTHEW 27:3-5)

AFTER THE SANHEDRIN found Jesus guilty and worthy of death, Judas Iscariot was overcome with remorse for having betrayed him. Judas sought to return the money to the priests who had paid him to betray Jesus. In observing Judas, we can see what repentance looks like: an intense grief over one's sin and a desire to make things right. However, Judas became convinced that he could not make things right. He was complicit in the impending death of Jesus. Judas could see only one way out: suicide.

Suicide is never, of course, the right way out. I have ministered with several families following a suicide. My own grandmother took her life before I was born. Her suicide had such negative ripple effects on her entire family. But she could not see this at the time. She actually felt that her course of action would make things better. It did not. Based on suicide letters I have read, it is clear that some who contemplate taking their own life lose the ability to see beyond their current situation. Judas could not see past the likely crucifixion of Jesus.

What would have happened if Judas had waited just three days before taking his own life? Had he waited three days, he would have seen the other side of his betrayal. He would have seen

Jesus raised from the dead. Had he seen the risen Christ and fallen on his knees at Jesus' feet, asking for mercy, what do you think Jesus would have said? There is no doubt he would have forgiven Judas. Now imagine the witness Judas would have had if he had just waited three days. You can almost hear him preaching: "I so loved the things of this world and so believed in the spirit of the revolution against Rome that I actually sold Jesus out for thirty pieces of silver. But I'm here to tell you today that the grave could not hold him down! And after his resurrection, he forgave even me. If he could forgive me for the terrible thing I did, don't you know that his grace is sufficient for you?

Judas would have become one of the most powerful witnesses for Christ, had he only waited three days.

The third day—the day when hope breaks through your darkness—always comes. The psalmist noted, "Weeping may linger for the night, but joy comes with the morning" (Psalm 30:5). So trust hard, and remember the story of Judas. Regardless of where you have been, Christ is able and willing to forgive you and to give you a new future with hope.

> *Lord, at times I, like Judas, have betrayed you by my actions. Forgive me, I pray. In those moments when life seems hopeless, may I remember the tragic end of Judas' life and the story of your resurrection; and help me to trust in you. Amen.*

21. Where Were the Dissenters?

Then the high priest tore his clothes and said, "Why do we still need witnesses? You have heard his blasphemy! What is your decision?" All of them condemned him as deserving death. (MARK 14:63-64)

MARK TELLS US THAT Joseph of Arimathea was a "respected member of the council" (Mark 15:43). John tells us that Nicodemus was a "leader of the Jews" (John3:1), which likely meant that he too was a member of the Sanhedrin. Both men were sympathetic toward Jesus. In John 3 we read that Nicodemus met Jesus at night for a conversation in which Jesus told him that he must be "born from above"

(John 3:3). Nicodemus came to Jesus at night for fear of what the other members of the council would say about his interest in the teachings of Jesus. John notes that Joseph "was a disciple of Jesus, though a secret one because of his fear of the Jews" (John 19:38).

Presumably, these two men were at the trial of Jesus early Friday morning. Although Luke does report that "Joseph...had not agreed to their plan and action" (Luke 23:50-51), none of the four Gospels records dissenting arguments by any of the seventy-one Sanhedrin members. Why didn't Nicodemus or Joseph speak up for Jesus?

Several years ago a man sent me an e-mail detailing a sermon he had heard as a boy some forty years before but had never forgotten. He had attended a small, rural church where the preacher that day had been the lay leader, a big man with a booming voice and a gentle spirit. The sermon was called "Standing on the Edge of the Crowd." In it, the lay leader described an experience he had had in the 1920s. A crowd had gathered on the edge of town, and he had gone to see what was happening. In the center of the crowd was a young black man who was about to be hanged. In his sermon the lay leader described his feelings as he watched the lynching, repulsed by it and knowing how wrong it was, yet too afraid to stand up against the crowd. The image of the young man being hanged and the memory of his own silence haunted this man forty years after the event.

Joseph and Nicodemus were respected leaders who were afraid to let others know they were sympathetic to Jesus and who seem to have stood by in silence as he was condemned to die. Are you willing to stand up and speak out when you see something you know in your heart is wrong? Or do you silently acquiesce to the crowd?

*Lord, forgive me for the times when I have gone
along with the crowd rather than stand up for
others or for what I believed was right. Give me
the courage to speak up when injustice is being
done. Amen.*

22. On Trial Before Pontius Pilate

They bound Jesus, led him away, and handed him over to Pilate. Pilate asked him, "Are you the King of the Jews?" He answered him, "You say so." Then the chief priests accused him of many things. Pilate asked him again, "Have you no answer? See how many charges they bring against you." But Jesus made no further reply, so that Pilate was amazed. (MARK 15:1b-5)

PONTIUS PILATE RULED AS governor of Judea from AD 26 to AD 36 or early 37. We know little about him. Josephus, the first-century Jewish historian, recorded several stories describing conflicts between Pilate and the people he governed which ultimately resulted in

Pilate being recalled to Rome. Philo of Alexandria described Pilate as cruel, corrupt, and violent.

Nevertheless, early that Friday morning the Temple guard, followed by the members of the Sanhedrin, led the bound Jesus through the streets of Jerusalem to the governor's palace. There they presented him to the governor, charging him with the capital offense of claiming to be a king—a crime tantamount to treason and insurrection.

It was most unusual for the Jewish ruling council to bring to the Roman governor an individual they wished for Rome to execute. Pilate saw through their apparent interest in upholding Rome's authority. He knew that they tolerated Rome's authority and accommodated to it, but their presentation of Jesus to him was not out of a concern for Rome. Pilate knew they were jealous of this man who had challenged not Rome's authority, but their own. As Jesus stood before

Pilate, he refused to respond to the accusations they made against him. Pilate was surprised by Jesus' silence. Why didn't he defend himself against the charges of the priests? Some see his silence as another occasion when Jesus was intentionally fulfilling the words of the prophets, in this case Isaiah 53:7:

> *He was oppressed, and he was afflicted,*
> *yet he did not open his mouth;*
> *like a lamb that is led to the slaughter;*
> *and like a sheep that before its shearers is silent,*
> *so he did not open his mouth.*

When you think of Jesus standing silently before Pilate and his accusers, how do you picture him? What expression might have crossed his face as he heard the charges?

I picture dignity; resolve; a certain righteous disdain for the high priest; and an awareness that the trial will end in his own death, regardless of what he says, and that God will use his death to change the world forever.

Jesus was king of the Jews. At his birth, wise men came from the east seeking him. Likewise, shepherds hurried to Bethlehem to see the newborn king. As he stood before the priests and the Roman governor, Jesus was preparing for his impending coronation.

> *Lord, though you were rejected by the Sanhedrin and crucified by Rome, I hail you as my King. Help me faithfully to follow you wherever you may lead. Amen.*

23. A Choice Between Two Saviors

Now at the festival the governor was accustomed to release a prisoner for the crowd, anyone whom they wanted. At that time they had a notorious prisoner, called Jesus Barabbas. So after they had gathered, Pilate said to them, "Whom do you want me to release for you, Jesus Barabbas or Jesus who is called the Messiah?"(MATTHEW 27:15-17)

BY THE TIME PILATE HAD finished his initial examination of Jesus, he had learned that the kingdom Jesus sought to lead was "not of this world." Jesus was interested in the reign of God within the hearts and lives of God's people. Perhaps Pilate had learned that Jesus had taught his followers to love their enemies. Maybe Pilate had heard that Jesus had taught them to turn the other cheek. If Pilate knew nothing else, he certainly knew that the only revolt Jesus led was against the religious authorities and that this was why they were demanding his death.

Pilate had a practice every year at Passover aimed at keeping the peace in Jerusalem: He would free one political prisoner of the people's choosing. This year he would give the people a choice. He would either free a notorious criminal—a murderer and thug who had sought to lead a revolt against Rome—or he would free Jesus of Nazareth, whom the multitudes had welcomed with open arms into Jerusalem.

While Pilate was examining Jesus, a crowd had gathered outside the praetorium. Pilate brought Jesus before the crowd, and he offered them the opportunity to choose Barabbas or Jesus for release.

Matthew's Gospel notes that Barabbas' name was actually Jesus Barabbas. Remember that the name Jesus meant "savior," or "God saves." Barabbas meant "son of the father." So we could say that Pilate offered the crowd a choice between two saviors. Jesus Barabbas sought to lead a rebellion against Rome using violence and terror to rid the land of Romans. Jesus of Nazareth sought to lead people to "seek...first the kingdom of God" (Matthew 6:33, KJV); and he called his followers to love their enemies.

On this Friday morning the crowd made their choice: Barabbas. They asked that Pilate free a notorious criminal who had demonstrated his willingness to take up arms against the Romans. In the two thousand years since that day, human beings have been faced again and again with the choice between violence and love. We have found it easier to resort to violence than to love our enemies. Given the choice between a leader who is perceived as strong and willing to use force and one who advocates following the teachings of Jesus in dealing with our enemies, which would most people choose today?

> *Lord, help me to turn the other cheek and love*
> *my enemies. Today I pray for peace in our*
> *world. Guide our leaders to work for justice and*
> *peace. Help us to choose your path over that of*
> *Barabbas. Amen.*

24. The Conscience of a Spouse

While [Pilate] was sitting on the judgment seat, his wife sent word to him, "Have nothing to do with that innocent man, for today I have suffered a great deal because of a dream about him." (MATTHEW 27:19)

THE NEW TESTAMENT DOES not give us the name of Pontius Pilate's wife, though the traditions of the third-century church call her Procula (and much later she is identified by the name Claudia or Claudia Procula). The Eastern Orthodox Church recognizes her as a saint, as does the Ethiopian Church.

In a sense she played the role in the New Testament of Esther in the Old Testament. Esther was the wife of King Ahasuerus (also known as Xerxes) of Persia. Esther's husband had already deposed one queen for standing up to him and opposing his wishes. Further, there was a law that extended the death penalty to anyone who approached the king's throne without being invited. But when Esther learned that the king had signed a decree that would result in the complete annihilation of all the Jews, she courageously pleaded the case of her people; and as a result they were saved. Esther is remembered every year at the Jewish festival of Purim for her courage in standing up for justice and for her people.

Procula was the Roman wife of Pontius Pilate. Her powerful husband held the fate of the Son of God in his hands. Procula did not know the identity of Jesus; but she had been troubled in her dreams about him, and she knew he was not guilty. She sent word to Pilate to have "nothing to do with that innocent man" (Matthew 27:19).

Such interference in an official trial must have been most remarkable and required courage on Procula's part. Yet unlike King Ahasuerus, who took seriously the counsel of his wife Esther, Pilate did not heed Procula's words.

In the Book of Esther it was Haman, one of the king's nobles, who wished to destroy the Jewish people. His wife, Zesher, far from standing up to her husband and calling him to do what was right, actually encouraged him in his sin. She stood in stark contrast to the righteous Esther.

Married persons must understand that part of the call from God in marriage is to help your spouse do the right and just thing. Are you willing to confront your mate and speak up when he or she is considering an action that will harm others, even if your words might result in conflict with your mate? Further, are you open to hearing your mate when he or she challenges your actions or decisions? King Ahasuerus was, and he will

be forever remembered for retracting his edict.
Pontius Pilate refused to heed the words of his
wife, and he will be forever remembered for the
resulting action.

> *Lord, help me to have the courage of Esther and*
> *Procula by speaking up in the face of wrong.*
> *Give me the wisdom of Ahasuerus, who listened*
> *to his mate and changed his course of action as*
> *a result. Teach me courage and humility. Amen.*

25. The Examination by Herod

He sent [Jesus] off to Herod [Antipas], who was himself in Jerusalem at that time. When Herod saw Jesus, he was very glad, for he had been wanting to see him for a long time, because he had heard about him and was hoping to see him perform some sign. He questioned him at some length, but Jesus gave him no answer. The chief priests and the scribes stood by, vehemently accusing him. Even Herod with his soldiers treated him with contempt and mocked him; then he put an elegant robe on him, and sent him back to Pilate. (LUKE 23:7-11)

PILATE KNEW THAT EXECUTING Jesus was unjust. It was for this reason that, upon hearing that Herod Antipas was in Jerusalem, he decided to send Jesus to Herod to decide the case. Herod ruled over the Galilee which, Pilate reasoned, gave Herod ultimate responsibility for the case, since Jesus was a Galilean.

When Herod the Great died in 4 BC, he was unwilling to leave his entire kingdom to just one of his sons; so he divided it into four parts. He left the northern region of Galilee to his son Herod Antipas but refused to give him the title "king." Antipas would thus rule as "tetrarch" over Jesus' home territory for forty-two years before being deposed by Emperor Caligula and sent into exile. Besides his part in the trial of Jesus, Herod Antipas is known in the Gospels for executing Jesus' cousin John the Baptist. In the case of John the Baptist, we are told that Herod did not want to kill him; but when Herod's half brother's daughter, at the prompting of her mother who was now married to Herod, requested the head of John the Baptist, Herod was unwilling to say no. In today's Scripture, Jesus stood before Herod Antipas; and the Sanhedrin wished him dead. Once again

Herod was unwilling to say no, but this time he avoided saying yes. He simply refused to accept jurisdiction and returned Jesus to Pilate.

The events of that first hour after sunrise on what we now call Good Friday occurred like this: Jesus was tried before the Sanhedrin, who wished to see him put to death but needed Pontius Pilate, the Roman governor, to take responsibility for that death. Pilate gave Jesus a brief trial but did not wish to accept responsibility for his death. Pilate then delivered Jesus to Herod Antipas, who was in Jerusalem for the Passover. Herod questioned Jesus but did not wish to take responsibility for his death; and so, after mocking Jesus, Herod sent him back to Pilate.

Neither of these rulers wanted to take responsibility, yet each ultimately was responsible; for Pilate and Herod each had the power to stop the Crucifixion, but they refused. Failing to stop a wrong is itself morally wrong.

Are there times when, like Herod, you could have spoken out to stop a wrong but refused?

Lord, you know the moments when I should have spoken up but was silent. You know when I have passed the blame to another and failed to take responsibility for my part in a wrong done. Help me not to blame, but instead to act in preventing wrong before it happens. Amen.

26. What Is Truth?

Then Pilate entered the headquarters again, summoned Jesus, and asked him, "Are you the King of the Jews?" Jesus answered, "Do you ask this on your own, or did others tell you about me?" Pilate replied, "I am not a Jew, am I? Your own nation and the chief priests have handed you over to me. What have you done?" Jesus answered, "My kingdom is not from this world. If my kingdom were from this world, my followers would be fighting to keep me from being handed over to the Jews. But as it is, my kingdom is not from here." Pilate asked him, "So you are a king?" Jesus answered, "You say that I am a king. For this I was born, and for this I came into the world, to testify to the truth. Everyone who belongs to the truth listens to my voice." Pilate asked him, "What is truth?" (JOHN 18:33-38)

LEARNING THAT HEROD WOULD not pronounce judgment on Jesus, Pilate summoned Jesus before the judgment seat once more. Pilate asked him, in essence, "Are you leading a rebellion? Do you fancy yourself the king of the Jews? And if not, what is it that you have done to turn the Sanhedrin against you?" Jesus' response is important: "My kingdom is not from this world."

Jesus came preaching, "The kingdom of God is among you" (Luke 17:21). The kingdom of God was the primary focus of his teaching, preaching, and ministry. In a world of kings and tetrarchs and emperors, the significance of God's kingdom was clear. There was Caesar's kingdom (and all the other kingdoms of this world), and there was God's kingdom. Jesus called his followers to live as citizens of two kingdoms: the earthly kingdom, where they paid their taxes, loved their enemies, and served even their Roman oppressors with dignity, and God's kingdom, where they sought to do God's will. They were to pray earnestly, "Thy kingdom come, thy will be done, on earth as it is in heaven."

Jesus' ministry was devoted to helping his followers see, hear, and understand what it meant to hail God as King. He described the King in terms that were unforgettable (like a father who welcomes back the prodigal son). He taught what the King required of his subjects (to love the Lord and love one's neighbor as oneself). He described the King's priorities (The first will be last, and the last will be first.) and the King's criterion for greatness (Act as servants rather than insist on being served.). Pilate asked, "So you are a king?" Jesus answered, "For this I was born, and for this I came into the world, to testify to the truth. Everyone who belongs to the truth listens to my voice." Pilate then asked, "What is truth?" (See John 18:37-38.) Philosophers have debated that question for centuries, yet in this case the setting made the question deeply ironic. Pilate was standing in the presence of truth personified, truth incarnate, the very source of truth about God and humanity and the purpose of life. The font of truth was bound hand and foot, preparing to be tortured and crucified.

> *Lord, I wish to live as a subject in your kingdom.*
> *Reign in my life. May your kingdom come and*
> *your will be done on earth as it is in heaven.*
> *May your words and your life be the defining*
> *truth of my life. Amen.*

27. The Shout of the Crowd

Pilate said to [the crowd], "Then what should I do with Jesus who is called the Messiah?" All of them said, "Let him be crucified!" Then he asked, "Why, what evil has he done?" But they shouted all the more, "Let him be crucified!"

So when Pilate saw that he could do nothing, but rather that a riot was beginning, he took some water and washed his hands before the crowd, saying, "I am innocent of this man's blood; see to it yourselves." Then the people as a whole answered, "His blood be on us and on our children!" (MATTHEW 27:22-25)

PILATE IS PORTRAYED IN almost sympathetic terms in the Gospels as he tried to convince the crowd gathered outside the praetorium that Jesus was innocent. Likewise the crowd gathered there is portrayed as bloodthirsty and on the verge of riot.

Unfortunately, the Gospel accounts of the trial have been at times used as the basis for justifying anti-Semitism and atrocities against the Jewish people. This particular passage was a source of debate surrounding Mel Gibson's film *The Passion of the Christ*. Some were concerned that the words "His blood be on us and on our children!" might bring about a resurgence of anti-Semitism.

In the community where my church is located, Jews were not permitted to own homes well into the 1960s. The city limits were actually redrawn to exclude a neighborhood where several Jewish families lived. How is it that the followers of Jesus could come to act in such unChristlike ways?

When we read the story of the crowd shouting "Crucify him!" we are meant to remember several things: (1) Jesus and nearly everyone in the earliest church were Jews; (2) some of the crowd members were most likely merchants whose tables Jesus had overturned earlier in the week, and certainly not all the Jews in Jerusalem were present; and (3) if we look, we can see ourselves in the crowd.

There is an evil that lurks within all of us, a capacity to hate and an ability to participate in hateful activities. I am reminded of the interviews Jean Hatzfeld conducted for his book *Machete Season*. Hatzfeld interviewed ten Hutu men who were in prison for crimes committed during the 1994 genocide in Rwanda, when Hutu countrymen killed as many as a million of their Tutsi neighbors over the course of just a hundred days. What is so disturbing about Hatzfeld's interviews with these killers is that they show just how easy it was for ordinary human beings to set aside their humanity and commit terrible acts against others.

When Luke tells us that Pilate petitioned the crowd three times in the hope of releasing Jesus, we are reminded of other significant events in the Gospels. Three times Jesus was tempted by the devil. Three times the disciples fell asleep in the garden. Three times Peter denied knowing Jesus. Three times the crowd, when told of the innocence of Jesus, cried out, "Crucify him!" And three times Pilate could have said, "I refuse to crucify an innocent man." But he did not.

What darkness do you see in your own soul? Bigotry? Hatred? Anger when your sin is exposed? Frustration when others do not see eye to eye with you? Can you see yourself in the crowd?

Lord, help us see the darkness that lurks in our souls. By your Spirit change us, that we might overcome our fear and hate with faith and love. Amen.

28. Wishing to Satisfy the Crowd

So Pilate, wishing to satisfy the crowd, released Barabbas for them; and after flogging Jesus, he handed him over to be crucified. (MARK 15:15)

PERHAPS NOWHERE IN HUMAN history have more tragic words been written of an individual than those Mark wrote when he said that Pilate, "wishing to satisfy the crowd," sent Jesus to be crucified. Pilate did not order Jesus' crucifixion because he felt Jesus was guilty of a crime worthy of death—in fact, just the opposite. Pilate was certain Jesus was not guilty. Pilate had the authority and power to set Jesus free but refused to exercise it. Instead, *wishing to satisfy the crowd*, he sent Jesus to be crucified.

Why did Pilate wish to satisfy the crowd? Was it merely that he feared a rebellion if he did not crucify Jesus? Perhaps. Did he want to accommodate the crowd because he was tired of dealing with Jesus? Probably. Was it even possible that, like many of us, Pilate wanted the crowd to accept and affirm him? It seems unlikely, based on what we know about Pilate, a cruel man who routinely abused his subjects. And yet, I wonder.

I am fundamentally a people pleaser. Most pastors are. We are wired to like people and to want them to like us. I suspect the same is true of politicians as well. Maybe it is also true of you. What happens when you are faced with doing something you believe is right but which will cause a large number of people to be upset with you, maybe even turn against you? I have felt this regarding my preaching, knowing that if I preached this or that sermon or came out in this or that place on an issue, people would leave our church. I came to realize some time ago just how easy it is to betray God, even to lose your soul, if your primary objective is to satisfy the crowd.

Pilate gave in to the demands of the crowd and sent the Son of God to be tortured and crucified. When have you said or done things aimed at satisfying the crowd? When have you remained silent when you should have spoken out?

Lord, you know every time I have had a crisis of courage. You know when I have been silent and when I should have spoken out. Forgive me; and teach me boldness, courage, and love. Amen.

29. The Flogging

Then Pilate took Jesus and had him flogged.
(JOHN 19:1)

THE GOSPELS TELL US LITTLE about the form Jesus' flogging took. Far more time is devoted to describing the humiliation he endured at the hands of the soldiers. We know from reading other sources, however, that on occasion persons died in the midst of being beaten by the Roman "lictors" with their whips and rods. These sources also tell us that the flesh was torn from the bones when the guards used whips whose leather was embedded with sharp objects. This was a serious punishment for wrongdoing. But for whose wrongdoing was Jesus being punished?

Isaiah 53 is known as a "suffering servant" passage. Some believe that the suffering servant of Isaiah was the nation of Israel personified, being punished for the individual sins of her people as she was led into exile. The early church found in this and other passages a prefiguring and prophetic picture of what happened to Jesus on the cross. In Isaiah 53:5 we read:

> *He was wounded for our transgressions,*
> *crushed for our iniquities;*
> *upon him was the punishment that made us whole,*
> *and by his bruises we are healed.*

When I was a child, my parents would occasionally spank me, demanding that I hand over my belt so they could use it for the punishment. These spankings were seldom painful. My mother was always upset in giving this punishment, but she had been taught by her parents (who learned it from the Bible) that to "spare the rod" was to "spoil the child." When she had finished, she would hug me and tell me she loved me. She considered the spanking necessary so I would learn to lay aside the misdeed; but ultimately her aim was not punishment, but restoration, healing, and character development.

The suffering and death of Jesus can be seen through many different lenses. One of these is the lens of punishment and forgiveness. Jesus volunteered to take upon himself a punishment that rightly belonged to us. As described in Isaiah, "he was wounded for our transgressions" and "by his bruises we are healed."

Lord, help me to comprehend fully what it means to say that you were wounded for my transgressions and crushed for my iniquities. Amen.

30. The Humiliation of the King

Then the soldiers led him into the courtyard of the palace (that is, the governor's headquarters); and they called together the whole cohort. And they clothed him in a purple cloak; and after twisting some thorns into a crown, they put it on him. And they began saluting him, "Hail, King of the Jews!" They struck his head with a reed, spat upon him, and knelt down in homage to him.

(MARK 15:16-19)

THERE ARE MANY DIFFERENT dimensions to the suffering and death of Jesus Christ. Among them is the idea that in Jesus' suffering and death, God was fully identifying with us and was able to experience what we go through as human beings. God knows what it means to feel small, to be attacked mentally and emotionally, and to be physically abused.

Matthew, Mark, and John tell us of the humiliation Jesus experienced at the hands of the Roman soldiers. He was taken before the entire cohort—some three hundred to six hundred soldiers—who stripped him naked, mocked him, crowned him with thorns, struck him, and spat upon him. He stood there naked, accepting the meanness, the hate, the cruelty. I envision his strength, staring at his tormentors with determination and perhaps even a glint of pity. He took their spittle, their blows, their taunts.

I am reminded of a girl in my third-grade class at Prairie Elementary School. I do not know why she was picked on, but picked on she was. I remember walking out on the playground one day and seeing her sitting there, surrounded by kids who were teasing and taunting her. This continued over the course of a semester; and though I do not recall joining in, I know I never stood up for her. By the end of the semester, she was no longer in our school. It is not only Roman soldiers who know how to be cruel and inhumane.

For every child who was ever picked on, taunted, and humiliated, Jesus stood there that day. For every man and woman who was ever made to feel small by others, he stood there that day. For every victim of torture, everyone falsely condemned, everyone who has been abused by another, he stood there as if God were saying, "I subjected myself to the hate and meanness of others so that I could identify with you."

Lord, my heart aches as I imagine you standing among the soldiers as they hurled insults and spat upon you. Thank you for enduring shame so that you might know the pain we human beings sometimes experience. Thank you for identifying with our hurt and pain. Forgive me for those times when I have been on the giving end of this hurt, when by my words and actions I made others feel small. Amen.

31. They Compelled Simon to Carry His Cross

They compelled a passer-by, who was coming in from the country, to carry his cross; it was Simon of Cyrene, the father of Alexander and Rufus. (MARK 15:21)

IT IS A FIVE-MINUTE WALK between the traditional site of Jesus' sentencing and Golgotha, where he was crucified. But for a man beaten nearly to death and forced to carry the seventy-five-pound *patibula* (the horizontal beam of the cross), this could have taken a half-hour. When Jesus could not carry his cross any farther, a man named Simon was enlisted to carry the cross the rest of the way to Golgotha.

Simon was not a follower of Jesus. He was merely a "passer-by." He had come to Jerusalem to celebrate the Passover and probably had many things to do that day as he made his way through the streets of the Holy City. And then it happened: He was seized by a Roman soldier and pressed into service, forced to carry the beam of a convicted man's cross.

Frightened and perhaps frustrated, Simon picked up the beam, slung it over his shoulder, balanced it there, and then sought to help the bloodied and beaten man. The sooner he reached Golgotha, the sooner he could leave, go back to his tasks, and forget about the entire experience.

What Simon did not know was that this unexpected interruption to his otherwise busy day would ultimately be the most profound and important experience of his entire life. For in this interruption he had carried the cross for the King of Glory.

I have learned to pay attention to interruptions. I was disembarking from a plane in Nashville, Tennessee, when I saw a woman I knew sitting in a wheelchair, with medical personnel attending her. I stopped to see if I could help, and she assured me she was OK and that I should go on. The medics indicated that she would be fine, and I started to leave; but something told me I should stay. I spent the next couple of hours with her, ultimately encouraging her to go to the hospital. At first she refused, but later she went on her own. The next night she called me from a hospital room saying, "Your encouragement to go to the hospital may have saved my life." This interruption was more important than the work I had come to Nashville to do.

It is likely that Simon went on to become a follower of Christ. Mark mentioned him and his sons, Alexander and Rufus, in a matter-of-fact fashion, assuming the Christians at Rome (the likely recipients of his Gospel) would know them. They were likely leading figures of the church there. In that frightening and burdensome interruption of Good Friday, Simon's life would forever be changed.

> *Lord, help me pay attention to the interruptions and to see in them opportunities to serve you and do your will. Amen.*

32. The Crucifixion

It was nine o'clock in the morning when they crucified him. The inscription of the charge against him read, "The King of the Jews." (MARK 15:25-26)

WITH THE CRUCIFIXION OF Jesus, we reach the climax of the story by which God intends to save the world. Every detail has meaning. It is filled with pathos and irony. It is bad news, for in it we see the Son crucified and human beings at their very worst. Yet at the same time it is good news; for it reveals God's suffering with us and for us, his redemption of humankind, and ultimately the full extent of his love.

Mark's description of the Crucifixion is sparse; he did not go into the details that some modern films have presented. Mark simply says, "They crucified him" (Mark 15:25). It was not necessary for Mark to describe crucifixion to the Christians at Rome because they had seen the hideous sight on many occasions. They knew why Cicero called it the "cruelest and most disgusting penalty."

Since we modern readers have not seen crucifixions, our images of Jesus' crucifixion typically come from sacred art. But today we know that some of the details captured on canvas, in sculpture, or on film are likely inaccurate. Let's correct a few of those.

Jesus is usually portrayed on the cross wearing a loincloth. But it is likely that he was crucified naked. The Romans wished not merely to kill the victims or even simply to torture them; they intended to humiliate them as well. We typically picture Jesus' feet nailed one on top of the other at the front of the cross; but the bones of a crucifixion victim discovered in Jerusalem indicate that nails were driven through the side of the foot, around the heel bone. Each foot was nailed to the opposing side of the cross, the right foot to the right side and the left foot to the left side, so that the victim's legs straddled the cross. Jesus is usually pictured hanging on a cross that towers over those standing below, but Roman crosses were seldom more than six to nine feet tall from top to bottom. This means that when Jesus was crucified, his feet were probably only two feet off the ground. Imagine someone standing on a chair before you; this was the proximity of Mary to her son as he hung on the cross. As she stood by for six hours, she could have touched his hands and looked up into his eyes.

The Romans intended to humiliate Jesus. But John describes his crucifixion not as humiliation, but as glorification. This King of the Jews hung there, naked and suffering, to save his people. He laid down his life for them. It was here that God demonstrated his true character to the human

race, his willingness to suffer and die to save his
people.

> *Lord, I cannot fully comprehend the humiliation
> and suffering you endured on the cross.
> Nevertheless, help me to understand and be
> affected by this story. Help me to tremble at the
> thought of the One who loves me giving his life
> that I might live. Amen.*

33. Father, Forgive Them

Then two bandits were crucified with him, one on his right and one on his left. Those who passed by derided him, shaking their heads and saying, "You who would destroy the temple and build it in three days, save yourself! If you are the Son of God, come down from the cross." In the same way the chief priests also, along with the scribes and elders, were mocking him, saying, "He saved others; he cannot save himself. He is the King of Israel; let him come down from the cross now, and we will believe in him. He trusts in God; let God deliver him now, if he wants to; for he said, 'I am God's Son.'" The bandits who were crucified with him also taunted him in the same way. (MATTHEW 27:38-44)

WHEN JESUS WAS CRUCIFIED, those passing by derided him. The religious leaders mocked him. In Matthew's account even the thieves crucified on either side of him taunted him. Jesus hung bleeding, naked, dying; yet there was no compassion, only the cruelty of words meant to break his spirit. In essence the people said, "You who thought you were really some-thing—look at you now! You spoke as though you were the Messiah; but now you are naked, humiliated, and dying. You are *nothing*."

As children we were taught to reply to the taunts of others, "Stick and stones may break my bones, but words will never hurt me." But the words of others did hurt us. They still do.

I have long since forgiven and forgotten most of the insults ever thrown my way, but a handful of them are harder to let go. About the time I think I have forgotten them, they resurface to stir up old feelings of anger or hurt or pain.

When we are insulted and harassed by oth-ers, we can turn to Jesus, who knows the pain that words can bring. When we are treated cruelly, when we are wrongly insulted, he understands.

What was Jesus feeling as the people hurled their insults? Did he want to argue with them? Did he wish to hurl insults back? Did he find himself angry and ready to call down fire from heaven to destroy them?

Jesus had taught his disciples, "Blessed are you when people revile you...and utter all kinds of evil against you" (Matthew 5:11). He had told them, "Love your enemies and pray for those who persecute you, so that you may be children of your Father in heaven" (Matthew 5:44-45). He had taught them to show mercy and to extend forgiveness. It was easy to say such things from the hillsides of Galilee, where large crowds flocked to hear him. It was quite another to say them when experiencing the cruelty of others. Yet, hanging from the cross, Jesus prayed, "Father, forgive them; for they do not know what they are doing" (Luke 23:34).

Jesus not only taught us how to face those who taunt us; he demonstrated it as he prayed from the cross.

> *Lord, I am sorry that you were forced to endure the insults of those who stood by your cross. But I am grateful that you understand what it is to be wounded by the words of others. Forgive me for the times my words have wounded others. Please help me to forgive those whose words have wounded me. Amen.*

34. Behold Your Mother

Meanwhile, standing near the cross of Jesus were his mother, and his mother's sister, Mary the wife of Clopas, and Mary Magdalene. When Jesus saw his mother and the disciple whom he loved standing beside her, he said to his mother, "Woman, here is your son." Then he said to the disciple, "Here is your mother." And from that hour the disciple took her into his own home.

(JOHN 19:25b-27)

JESUS WAS HER BELOVED son. From the time she felt the first stirrings of life in her womb, their souls were intertwined. As she held him in her arms, she loved him more than she had ever loved anyone in her life. As he grew, so did her love for this child she had brought into the world. He was a gift from God.

Yet in the back of Mary's mind, in her earliest memories as his mother, there were the words of Simeon, the old man who had spoken to her when she and Joseph brought Jesus to be circumcised eight days after his birth: "This child is destined for the falling and the rising of many in Israel, and to be a sign that will be opposed so that the inner thoughts of many will be revealed—and a sword will pierce your own soul too" (Luke 2:34-35).

As she stood at the cross, looking into her son's eyes, Mary finally understood Simeon's words. This was the sword the old man had spoken of, and how it pierced her soul! The pain was unbearable. She could hardly breathe. It was not enough that they were killing her son. The taunts were enough to make her scream. In that moment when she could stand it no more, when she thought she herself would die, Jesus looked at her and said, "Woman"; and then slowly moving his head toward his young apostle John, he added, "this now is your son." And turning to John, he said, "This now is your mother" (paraphrase of John 19:26-27).

As Jesus hung there, dying on the cross, seeing the agony in his mother's eyes, he asked John to care for her and asked Mary to care for him. Tradition has it that John fulfilled Jesus' wishes and cared for Mary for the rest of her days.

This scene at the cross is a call for us to follow Jesus' example in caring for our mothers, but it is more than that. It is a reminder of the sacrifice and suffering Mary made for us and for our salvation. No human being, aside from Jesus himself, did more to bring about our salvation than Mary. She bore the Christ Child, nurtured him, prayed for him, worried over him. She suffered more than any other human being as she watched her son tortured and crucified. The price of our salvation was not only the suffering and death of Jesus but also the agony and pain of his mother.

Lord, even in the midst of your suffering you were thinking not of yourself, but of your mother. I remember the terrible price she paid, that you might offer us your salvation. As you cared for your mother, help me to care for my parents. Amen.

35. Today You Will Be With Me in Paradise

One of the criminals who were hanged there kept deriding him and saying, "Are you not the Messiah? Save yourself and us!" But the other rebuked him, saying, "Do you not fear God, since you are under the same sentence of condemnation? And we indeed have been condemned justly, for we are getting what we deserve for our deeds, but this man has done nothing wrong." Then he said, "Jesus, remember me when you come into your kingdom." He replied, "Truly I tell you, today you will be with me in Paradise." (LUKE 23:39-43)

JESUS WAS CRUCIFIED between two criminals. There was something strangely fitting in this, for Jesus had spent most of his public ministry trying to reach people just such as these. As he once had told the Pharisees, "The Son of

Man came to seek out and to save the lost" (Luke 19:10). He had said, "Those who are well have no need of a physician, but those who are sick" (Mark 2:17). Even as he hung on the cross, Jesus showed the kind of compassion and concern for lost people that he had demonstrated throughout his ministry.

Both thieves initially joined the crowd and the religious leaders in mocking Jesus as he hung between them. But one of the men had a change of heart as he listened to Jesus' words from the cross. This thief spoke to Jesus, saying, "Remember me when you come into your kingdom" (Luke 23:42).Was the man simply offering kind words to Jesus; or did he truly understand that Jesus, by his death, was ushering in his kingdom? In either case, at that moment Jesus promised the man that he would join Jesus in paradise.

This criminal knew virtually nothing about Jesus' teachings. He had not been baptized.

Yet Jesus offered him *paradise*, based solely on the man's desire to be with Jesus in his eternal kingdom. What does this teach us about the grace of the Lord?

The word *paradise* originally signified a park or orchard. The Bible begins and ends in paradise. It begins with Eden, God's orchard. And it ends in Revelation 22 with a description of the heavenly kingdom—a picture of paradise. It was paradise that Jesus offered the thief on the cross.

Some years ago, a parishioner named Ruth told me about her grandmother, who had slipped into a coma days before her death. As the woman's life drew to a close, the family gathered around the bedside. Minutes before she died, she opened her eyes, sat up in bed, and looked right at her granddaughter. She smiled and said, "Ruth, it's absolutely beautiful." Then she lay down and died. Ruth, seventy years after this event, told me that since hearing her grandmother's words, she

never again had feared death. I believe that Ruth's
grandmother saw paradise.

> *Lord, I want to be with you in your kingdom.*
> *Please ready my heart, that when this life is*
> *over, I might be with you in paradise. Amen.*

36. Why Have You Forsaken Me?

When it was noon, darkness came over the whole land until three in the afternoon. At three o'clock Jesus cried out with a loud voice, "Eloi, Eloi, lema sabachthani?" which means, "My God, my God, why have you forsaken me?" (MARK 15:33-34)

Then Jesus, crying with a loud voice, said, "Father, into your hands I commend my spirit." (LUKE 23:46a)

"WHEN IT WAS NOON, darkness came over the whole land" (Mark 15:33). For three hours the darkness persisted. Two passages from Exodus come to mind when we read of this darkness. The first is the plague of darkness that came upon the land of the Egyptians, a plague meant to lead Pharaoh to set the Israelite slaves free. It is described in Exodus 10:21 as "a darkness that can be felt." But there is another darkness one might recall. In Exodus 20:21 we read that the presence of God was shrouded in "thick darkness." It was in the midst of this darkness that God made his covenant with Israel, through his servant Moses. Perhaps the darkness on the day of Jesus' crucifixion was an expression both of God's displeasure and anger over what had happened to his Son and of God's presence, at the cross, making a new covenant with humanity through Jesus Christ.

It was during the period of darkness, as Jesus' suffering on the cross drew to an end, that Matthew and Mark tell us Jesus offered what is often called the "cry of dereliction." Jesus spoke the words of Psalm 22:1: "My God, my God, why have you forsaken me?" That Jesus would quote these words points to the fact that he was meditating upon the psalms as he suffered on the cross. Psalm 22 is a "lament" or "complaint" psalm—one of many in which the psalmists expressed their feelings of disappointment or abandonment by God. The very fact that these psalms exist makes clear that even the most faithful people have moments when they feel forsaken by God. There are times when our life experience seems to negate, or at least to call into question, the goodness of God and even the existence of God.

I was recently talking with a man whose wife tragically died in an accident. The experience was so terribly painful. As we talked about God, the man began to weep and could not speak. Though he did not say what was on his mind, I could not help but feel that if he were to pray at that moment, he might have said, "My God, my God, why have you forsaken me?"

Does it help you to know that the Jesus you pray to in difficult times once cried out in disappointment, feeling forsaken by God? Do you think God had actually abandoned him? Psalm 22 and Jesus' prayer from the cross were actually words of faith. In the face of despair, both the psalmist and Jesus appealed to God. When one is surrounded by suffering and pain, even a cry of disappointment to God is an act of faith. It is this faith that we see in the last words of Jesus as described in Luke's Gospel. Following his cry of dereliction, Jesus uttered the prayer in which he entrusted his life to God: "Into your hands I commend my spirit" (Luke 23:46a).

Lord, there are times when I have felt forsaken too. Help me to call upon you in my hour of need. It comforts me to know that you understand what it is like to feel abandoned by God. Help me, in my moments of despair, to place my life in your hands. Amen.

37. I Thirst

After this, when Jesus knew that all was now finished,
he said (in order to fulfill the scripture), "I am thirsty."
A jar full of sour wine was standing there. So they put a
sponge full of the wine on a branch of hyssop and held it
to his mouth. (JOHN 19:28-29)

IT WAS HOLY WEEK, and I had been asked to
participate in a communitywide Good Friday
service based on the seven last words or state-
ments of Jesus from the cross. I had been assigned
the words *I am thirsty*. I had never thought much
about these words before.

That week, a mentor and good friend, Ray,
was dying. I went to see him and sit with him for
a while. During that time he turned to me and
said, "Adam, I'm thirsty." I carefully drew water

into a straw; held my finger on one end of the straw to prevent the water from draining out; and then placed the straw between Ray's lips, letting the water slowly trickle into his mouth. Repeating this act several times, I could not help but reflect on the words of Jesus from the cross. The words were a simple expression of Jesus' humanity. As death drew near, his mouth was dry and parched. He was thirsty.

But, like so much in John's Gospel, there is more here than might first meet the eye. In Jeremiah 2:13 and again in 17:13, God called himself "the fountain of living water." Jesus, picking up this idea in John 4, spoke to a Samaritan woman and offered her "living water" by which she would never be thirsty again. John's mention of Jesus' thirst on the cross is meant to be another glimpse into the tragedy and the sorrow of the Crucifixion. It is another way of pointing to the fact that in Jesus' death, the source of living water for all humankind was drying up, like a spring or well that has run dry.

I believe there is yet more to this story that John hoped we would notice. The Gospel of John tells us that someone offered Jesus a drink from a sponge as he spoke of his thirst. The sponge was filled with wine vinegar and placed on a branch of hyssop. The wine vinegar was sour and cheap. John's mention of this was likely included in part because in Psalm 69:21, the psalmist noted that his enemies gave him "vinegar to drink." John may have been pointing back to this psalm and seeing in it a prophecy of sorts. But more important than that was the image of the hyssop branch.

On the first Passover, the Israelites were instructed to dip a hyssop branch in the blood of the sacrificed lamb and then to use the hyssop to sprinkle the blood over their doorposts so that the angel of death would "pass over" their homes. Later, in Numbers and Leviticus, instructions were given for making persons ritually clean if they had been in contact with leprosy or with a dead body. Becoming ritually clean was achieved by mixing water with either bird's blood (in the case of leprosy) or ashes (in the case of contact with the dead) and then using a hyssop branch to sprinkle the individuals and their possessions with the watery mixture. Thus, hyssop was used to make persons clean and to protect the Israelites from death. It seems likely that John, in his account of the Crucifixion, was using the hyssop branch to point out the significance of Jesus' life and death. That is, by his blood Jesus was saving those who trust in him from death; and he was cleansing them from sin.

Lord, I remember today that you, who are the source of living water, thirsted on the cross. May I ever drink of your living water. Thank you for saving me from death and cleansing me from sin by your suffering and death. Amen.

38. It Is Finished

When Jesus had received the wine, he said, "It is finished." (JOHN 19:30a)

WHEN JESUS' LIFE drew to a close, John tells us that his final words were, "It is finished." What did Jesus mean by this? In one sense, his words were like "The End"—they simply marked the conclusion of the story of his suffering and death. But he meant more than that. The Greek word for "finished" (*teleos*) signifies an end toward which one has been working, a goal that has been accomplished or completed. Jesus' dying words tell us that he did not understand himself simply to be the victim of a tragic miscarriage of justice. Instead, in his death he had accomplished the mission for which God had sent him.

But what was the mission Jesus fulfilled by his death? Theologians have devoted volumes to answering this question. There are three broad directions their answers take. These three are not mutually exclusive but more likely complementary.

Let's consider the first of these today. It is sometimes called the "subjective" understanding of the Atonement. According to this view, the suffering and death of Jesus were meant to affect the human race deeply. Recall that John began his Gospel by saying that Jesus was God's Word become flesh. Jesus revealed God, and God's will for humanity, to us. As we have seen already, his suffering and death held a mirror to the human race to show us our brokenness and sin. But these events also revealed to us the love of a God who willingly suffered on our behalf in order to save us from ourselves and to win our hearts to him. Jesus' death changed how we see ourselves, God, and the world around us.

Several years ago, I saw a film that was so moving that when the screen faded to black and the words *The End* appeared, no one moved or spoke. Listening carefully, I could hear the sound of people weeping. When we rose to leave, somehow we were different because we had seen the film. The people in the audience left with a deep desire to be more courageous; to live selflessly and sacrificially; and, in the words of Proverbs 31:8, to "speak out for those who cannot speak, / for the rights of all the destitute." This is, in part, what Jesus accomplished for the human race when he said, "It is finished." The cross today moves us to understand the depth of God's love and the costliness of his work to save us.

The mission that Jesus had completed was, in part, to reveal to us our need for salvation; to show us the depth of God's love and mercy; and to call us, in turn, to lead lives of sacrificial love. In Jesus, God suffered for us that we might be saved.

As you imagine Jesus' suffering and death on the cross, how does the story affect you? What does it demand of you?

Lord, may I see in your crucifixion my sin, the depth of your love, and the costliness of your grace. Move me, that in response to your suffering I might learn to lay aside my sin and follow you with my whole heart. Help me to love sacrificially and to live faithfully as your disciple. Amen.

39. The Curtain...
Torn in Two

Then Jesus gave a loud cry and breathed his last. And the curtain of the temple was torn in two, from top to bottom. Now when the centurion, who stood facing him, saw that in this way he breathed his last, he said, "Truly this man was God's Son!" (MARK 15:37-39)

GOD, KNOWING THE Israelites would sin, made provision in the law for their restoration and healing through atoning sacrifices. The people were to bring a sacrificial offering to God as an expression of remorse, to make amends for their sin. The sacrifice was the worshiper's way of saying, "Lord, I am sorry for what I have done. This gift is a small token of my desire to be restored to right relationship with you."

God decreed a holy day for this purpose, called Yom Kippur, the Day of Atonement. On this day the high priest would use two goats to express national repentance, to atone for sins, and for the people to be restored to a right relationship with God. One goat would be sacrificed, and the blood would be taken inside the Holy of Holies (the throne room of God within the Temple). The entrance to the Holy of Holies was obscured by a large and heavy curtain through which the priest passed into the inner sanctum. There, before the "mercy seat" of God, he offered the blood with prayers for the people. The priest then laid his hands on the head of the second goat, symbolically placing the sins of the people there; and the goat was turned loose in the wilderness and driven from the people as a visible reminder that their sins had been sent away.

Jesus saw himself serving in the role of both high priest and sacrifice. He offered to God not the blood of a goat, but his own blood on behalf of the people. He said, in essence, "God, I give myself for these sinful, confused, and broken people. By the giving of my life, I ransom them. And by this sacrifice I mean for them to understand that their sins are forgiven." Jesus also served in the role of the goat turned loose in the wilderness. By offering his life to God, he demonstrated to humanity that mercy was extended to all.

When Matthew, Mark, and Luke describe the curtain of the Temple being torn in two, they mean for us to understand that Jesus has gone before the mercy seat of God, has made atonement for the sins of the human race, and has reconciled us to God.

Several years ago, a young man in the congregation I serve "hit bottom" after several years of running away from God, hurting himself, and hurting others. He walked into our empty sanctuary one afternoon and ran to the cross that hangs behind the choir loft, and there he wrapped his arms around the cross and wept. He understood in that moment that Jesus had borne the punishment he deserved and was the source of the mercy for which he longed.

Jesus offered himself to God on your behalf, and through his suffering and death he offers you grace.

> *Lord, I am sorry for the ways I fall short of God's will. Forgive my sins—those committed in thought, word, and deed, as well as those committed by my failure to do what God requires. Help me to live my life in grateful response to the gift of your salvation. Amen.*

40. The Burial

After these things, Joseph of Arimathea, who was a disciple of Jesus, though a secret one because of his fear of the Jews, asked Pilate to let him take away the body of Jesus. Pilate gave him permission; so he came and removed his body. Nicodemus, who had at first come to Jesus by night, also came, bringing a mixture of myrrh and aloes, weighing about a hundred pounds. They took the body of Jesus and wrapped it with the spices in linen cloths, according to the burial custom of the Jews. Now there was a garden in the place where he was crucified, and in the garden there was a new tomb in which no one had ever been laid. (JOHN 19:38-41)

AT ABOUT 3:00 PM Jesus died. Often the victims of crucifixion were left hanging on their crosses for days, as yet one more way of making of them examples so that others would not challenge Rome's laws or authority. But Joseph, a respected leader in Jerusalem, boldly asked for permission to bury Jesus; and Pilate agreed. Matthew tells us that Joseph laid Jesus to rest in his own tomb, newly hewn from the soft Jerusalem limestone. John tells us that this tomb was in a garden.

The burial and subsequent resurrection of Jesus points to yet another way of understanding the mission of Jesus as he died on the cross. On the cross, Jesus took all the evil that human beings could muster. He was persecuted by the righteous. He was tortured by the powerful. He was crucified unjustly. And finally, he died. On that Friday afternoon evil, sin, and death seemed to be victorious. Jesus would simply be one more in a long line of innocent and good men and women who had been unfairly killed.

The cross was a sign of injustice, jealousy, hatred, bigotry, abuse of power, and every other kind of sin. And on that day the forces of evil and sin defeated God and goodness and righteousness and life. Death, the great enemy that had reigned since Adam and Eve first turned away from God, had once more proven the victor. All that was left for Jesus' followers was grief, disillusionment, and despair.

Yet this was not the end of the story. The creed resounds with these powerful words: "On the third day, he rose from the dead"! Christians look at that terrible day when Christ died and call it Good Friday because we see it through the lens of the Resurrection. We know the rest of the story. We know that in the end, Jesus would dance on the head of death. We know that sin and evil and injustice and all the powers of hell were defeated on the cross and in the Resurrection.

At Jesus' burial, the forces of darkness seemed to have won. But on the third day, a different victory would come.

In our own lives, the forces of darkness often seem to hold the upper hand; but we remember that on the cross and at the Resurrection, Christ defeated evil and even death.

Lord, how grateful I am that your death and burial were not the end of the story! Help me remember, in those moments when darkness seems to have the upper hand, that you are the Victor! Help me to overcome my fear, even in the valley of the shadow of death. Amen.

Postscript:
In the Garden

Mary stood weeping outside the tomb. As she wept, she bent over to look into the tomb; and she saw two angels in white, sitting where the body of Jesus had been lying, one at the head and the other at the feet. They said to her, "Woman, why are you weeping?" She said to them, "They have taken away my Lord, and I do not know where they have laid him." When she had said this, she turned around and saw Jesus standing there, but she did not know that it was Jesus. Jesus said to her, "Woman, why are you weeping? Whom are you looking for?" Supposing him to be the gardener, she said to him, "Sir, if you have carried him away, tell me where you have laid him, and I will take him away." Jesus said to her, "Mary!" She turned and said to him in Hebrew, "Rabbouni!"

(JOHN 20:11-16)

THERE ARE MOMENTS in life so terrible, so painful, and so difficult that God's silence, or apparent absence, in the face of them leads us to question his very existence. I have ministered with families in the midst of terrible tragedies—automobile accidents, suicides, even murders. These people wanted to believe in God and in God's care for their loved ones. But the loss they had experienced was so terrible it seemed to negate the existence of God. Their pain seemed to proclaim, "If there is a God, this never would have happened!"

Mary must have experienced these feelings as she stood weeping outside the tomb that first Easter morning. She had watched all the events of the last twenty-four hours of Jesus' life. She was there at the cross as he breathed his last. Her faith in a God of goodness and love was shaken, if not completely shattered.

But death was not the final word in Jesus' story. As Mary stood weeping, a man, dressed as a gardener, appeared. He spoke her name; and she turned and saw Jesus. In a moment everything changed! Life had conquered death, and hope had vanquished despair!

Jesus' resurrection is a sign of the power and ultimate victory of God. And it is a word of hope that in the face of evil, tragedy, and death, we need not fear. Jesus has promised, "Because I love, you shall live also."

One final thought as we conclude this devotional. John tells us that Jesus was crucified and buried in the midst of a garden (John 19:41–42). John is alluding to another garden, the garden of Eden, where Adam and Eve disobeyed God and Paradise was lost. John wants us to understand that what happened at Eden was reversed at Calvary.

Did you notice that in John's Gospel, Jesus appeared to Mary as a gardener as if to say, "I've begun the work of restoring the garden." Jesus sent his disciples to continue the work he began.

They were to restore the garden by going into all the world making disciples and teaching them the things he had taught them. He still bids us to restore this garden we live in by pulling out the weeds of injustice, hate, poverty, and self-centeredness and sowing seeds of compassion, mercy, and love.

For the last twenty years, I have ended each of my Easter sermons the same way. People ask me from time to time, "Do you really *believe* this story—about Jesus' suffering, death, and resurrection?" My response is always the same. I not only believe it, *I am counting on it.*

Jesus Christ, I put my trust in you. Forgive my sins. Wash me clean, and make me new. Thank you for the hope I find in you and for helping me to see the love of God. I wish to live as your disciple. Help me to follow you. Use me to do your will and your work in this world—to restore your garden. And when this life is over, may I forever be with you. Amen.